The Story of a Law Teacher

First Edition	2009
Reprint	2012
Reprint	**2015**

The Story of a Law Teacher

Memoirs of

Padmashree Prof. N.R. Madhava Menon

Recorded in Conversation with

Prof. S. Surya Prakash

This book is a publication of **LexisNexis®**
(A Division of Reed Elsevier India (Pvt) Ltd)
14th floor, Building No 10, Tower–B, DLF Cyber City, Phase-II,
Gurgaon–122002, Haryana, India.
Tel : + 91 124 4774444 Fax: + 91 124 4774100

Website : www.lexisnexis.co.in / E-mail : help.in@lexisnexis.com

---

N.R. Madhava Menon, *Turning Point,* First Edition, Reprint 2015

ISBN: 978-81-7534-818-9

Printed by: Sita Fine Arts, New Delhi

Printed and bound in India.

ACKNOWLEDGEMENTS

This is not the work done on a regular basis because neither the man nor the material was available at one place. A series of piecemeal interviews with and without recording devices and occasional telephonic conversations were the source material for this book. I wish to express gratitude to my friends Dr. U.L. Narayana and Smt. A. Aruna Sree Lakshmi for their help in transcripting the recorded conversations and typing. I am thankful to Prof. Balraj Chauhan, Vice-Chancellor, RMNLU, Lucknow and Prof. S.S. Singh, Director, NLIU, Bhopal for their encouragement for the successful completion of this work.

I am grateful to Justices V.R. Krishna Iyer, D.M. Dharmadhikari, K.T. Thomas, A.K. Patnaik, Dr. V.S. Maliamath, Professors David McQuoid–Mason, Frank Bloch, R. Venkata Rao, M.K. Balachandran, B.P. Panda, Senior Advocates Fali S. Nariman, K.K. Venugopal and many of the colleagues and friends of Prof. Menon who shared their experiences and enriched the biography. I am indebted to one and all who supported me in completing this work. I owe my thanks to my colleagues Dr. P.K. Shukla, Dr. Sanjay Yadav and Mr. Partho Pratima Sharma for their comments and valuable suggestions.

I express my thanks to Dr. Manish Arora (Dy. Director & Associate Professor, Amity Law School) Director, Universal Law Publishing Co. Pvt. Ltd., New Delhi for readily giving consent for the publication and bringing 'Turning Point' in a beautiful way.

I express my deepest gratitude to my wife Lakshmi and my sons Ravi and Chetan for their immense support in completing this work.

DR. S. SURYA PRAKASH

Bhopal

PRAYER OF A TEACHER

"Where the mind is without fear and the head is held high;
Where knowledge is free;
Where the world has not been broken up into fragments by narrow domestic walls;
Where words come out from the depth of truth;
Where tireless striving stretches its arms towards perfection;
Where the clean stream of reason has not lost its way into the dreary desert sand of dead habit;
Where the mind is led forward by thee into ever widening thought and action;
Into that heaven of freedom, my Father, let my country awake"

'Gurudev' Rabindranath Tagore
from GITANJALI

PREFACE

I deem it a privilege to have the association with Prof. N.R. Madhava Menon, The Living Legend of Law, so called by the International Bar Association. Prof. Menon is a great teacher, best administrator and a good human being. Simple living and high thinking are his virtues. When the disrepute of legal education was at its height and when in the yester years the Law Commission of India chaired by Justice Setalvad said that "the lawyers coming out of legal institutions were half baked parasites let loose on society", there was a turn around in the 1980s. Legal education in the National Law Schools became the most sought after course and best legal minds were presented to the Nation. The credit goes to Padma Shree Dr. N.R. Madhava Menon. He was the founder Director of the National Law School of India University, Bangalore, National University of Juridical Sciences, Kolkata and National Judicial Academy, Bhopal. It was the vision of one man who stood against all odds and brought the Indian Law Schools on the world legal map. He has always been a maverick. He has firm views on legal education. He says, 'it is no longer enough to produce only legal practitioners, but they have to be social engineers as well'.

In 2003, I was officiating as Director of National Law Institute University, Bhopal and I approached Prof. Menon to invite him to deliver some guest lectures on criminal law to our students when he was serving as Director of the National Judicial Academy, Bhopal. He asked me to put the subject of Criminal Law which he agreed to teach in the first hour *i.e.,* 9 A.M. so that he could come and take the classes before he resumed his regular work in the Academy. As I myself was taking the subject I had the privilege to share the class with him. It was a sort of co-operative teaching. In spite of his busy schedule he came and took the classes on almost on regular basis for which he refused to take any honorarium. That's the spirit of a teacher. For me it was a joy to take class along with Prof. Menon. Before coming to Bhopal I was his colleague for some time at NUJS, Kolkata. Fortunately, both of us came to Bhopal and joined different institutions in the city. As I enjoyed some freedom with him we used to have long conversations which enriched me and I learned more about legal education in India and abroad. There were occasions in which he unfolded many silent chapters in his life and I thought his life is inspirational as he is a Karma Yogi in real sense. His life is illustrative of the adage 'work is worship'. I enjoyed the freedom to see him at anytime in his office or at home without any formalities. I thought that the Turning Point of legal education in India should not be buried under the sands of time and I took the initiative and started recording the interviews in the most informal ways with a view to collect as much information as possible about various events in his life.

He is a visionary, sensitive at heart and genuinely struggling for justice through legal education. This has been the mission of his life. Though he advocated justice education, he is aware of the challenges to that goal in the era of liberalization. Whether it is Corporate law or Labour law, both need a human face in application for rendering justice to the people. He firmly believes that law is for the people. Having commitment to uphold the socio-economic rights of the citizens, he cautioned against the plea to do away with subsidies on food, health and education in favour of market economy as it is against the spirit of the Constitution. Once he thundered at a seminar in Vijayawada that "unbridled privatization would be an invitation for disaster. If subsidies are scrapped and the public distribution system done away with or the State neglected its duties in providing the basic health and educational needs of the people, courts would be justified in intervening and directing the Government to do its duty." His insistence was for striking a right balance between economic reforms and the rights of the citizens guaranteed under the constitution particularly when they had limited access to justice. His conviction has been that in the era of globalization, the influence of the market forces cannot be underestimated and the best way to protect the interests of the nation and its citizens is through excellence in legal education where socially sensitive lawyers and enlightened judges will guard the rights of all the citizens of India.

Appreciating the efforts of Dr. Menon in restructuring the legal profession through improving legal education, the International Bar Association honoured him with the 'Living Legend of Law' Award in 1994 followed by Rotary Club of Bangalore conferring an Award for Vocational Excellence. The Bar Council of India presented a 'Plaque of Honour' for his contribution to legal profession. The President of India on the Republic Day in 2003, honoured Prof. Menon with Padma Shree, the first such award to a law teacher in India. He is also an advisor to the Commonwealth Judicial Education Institute, Halifax, Canada and serves on the Board of Governors of the International Centre for Judicial Trainers. He is a life member of Global Alliance for Justice Education and Commonwealth Legal Education Association which explain his services in the field of law around the world.

This is a modest attempt to compress an epic into an epigram. The interviews, the telephonic talks and the email transactions have ultimately resulted in this form. The boy who saw God in a morsel of food to the Director of National Judicial Academy – the journey is very long with many ups and downs. The discipline, commitment for a purpose, missionary zeal, and the work culture made Prof. Menon a remarkable person and a great administrator. This book is not merely lifesketch of Prof. Menon, it is also the history of legal education during this time. I have tried my best to bring to the readers all important things about Prof. Menon. Still there may be some events missing or I might have missed some of the names who were associated with Prof. Menon. For any such shortcomings the responsibility is mine. His life itself is a message and a turning point in the history of legal education of India.

Dr. S. Surya Prakash

5th September, 2009

drssprakash@yahoo.co.in

INTRODUCTION : LOOKING BACK

Modern Indian legal education has a history of over one and half centuries. It has seen so many twists and turns in the passage of time. Legal education has its direct impact on the administration of justice and access to justice for people. The quality of justice depends upon the quality of law graduates produced by the universities and colleges. The mushroom growth of law colleges in 1970s and 1980s which has had an adverse impact on the administration of justice compelled the policy makers to take corrective steps to improve the quality of legal education in India. The starting of the National Law School, Bangalore is a part of this effort. In view of my association with the Bar Council of India in shaping legal education policies in the 1970s and '80s, I was asked to take up the task of building a model law school which I completed with some measure of success. I humbly submit that I am only an instrument chosen by the circumstances.

O.W.Holmes once said that the life of law has not been logic; it has been experience. In fact, the study of law is a life long process. Law is as large and complex as life itself. Learning of law has to be founded on ethical principles if law has to serve the goal of justice. Therefore, study of law will be meaningful only when studied in the context of social realities. In a developing multi-cultural country like India which is in the process of change, orientation to the social milieu in which law operates is a *sine qua non* for social engineering through law. In fact, legal education has to be re-christened as "Justice Education" if it were to reflect its true mission in society. As medical education is intended to promote HEALTH rather than merely to treat diseases, legal education should aim at promoting JUSTICE rather than just learning about dispute resolution. The study of law is a fascinating intellectual pursuit for the creative minds. It will further strengthen the democratic values and help to promote the constitutional goals of Justice, Liberty, Equality and Fraternity assuring the dignity of all citizens.

I feel happy that today the study of law has become one of the most sought after courses particularly in the National Law Schools, which it was not two decades ago. It is heartening to note that the students from Indian law schools are now competing with their counterparts from the best law schools in the world and are advancing the cause of justice everywhere. The graduates of the National Law Schools are getting offers from national and international law firms as well as from corporate sectors with very hefty salary packages at par with those of the graduates of IITs and IIMs.

No doubt law graduates have a much larger role to play in society. I am hopeful that the law graduates particularly from the National Law Schools will think beyond the corporate sector and play a decisive role in litigation in the trial courts as well. There is no doubt that India needs a steady supply of socially sensitive and professionally competent lawyers to provide justice to the vast millions of poor and to meet the unmet legal needs of weaker sections. Let all law colleges become National Law Schools in their mission and delivery of educational services; only lawyers with competence and commitment can deliver and it is the function of law schools to strive for competitive excellence in every department of professional education.

I know Prof. Surya Prakash for more than a decade and he impressed me with his hard work, honesty and integrity. I invited him to join the faculty of the National University of Juridical Sciences at Kolkata in 2001 but he stayed with me only for a short period. He was invited by late Shri S.B. Chavan to take charge of the Law College at Nanded, Maharashtra of which he was the Chairman. I advised him to take the assignment as a challenge and join Nanded as it will be a greater service if one can help improve quality of education in backward areas. Of course, his desire to work with talented students in competitive environments brought him back to the National Law School few years later, this time at NLIU at Bhopal.

Incidentally Surya Prakash's moving to Bhopal provided the occasion to resume our association when I joined National Judicial Academy, Bhopal. I greatly appreciate his frankness and straightforward approaches. With his amiable and endearing manners he used to ask enthusiastically many things about legal education and my own life. We thus came close to each other and interacted freely. Though I am hesitant to present a biography as I am only an ordinary teacher, he insisted that all the efforts I did to change the course of legal education should be recorded for posterity. Unfortunately, half way through I had to leave Bhopal due to ill health of my wife. However, his determination, perseverance and never-give-up attitude led to the sending of e-mails and long telephonic conversations which resulted in the completion of this work. I thank him for the effort which spread over several years.

May I take this opportunity to express my deep-felt gratitude to all my colleagues and friends and to generations of students who gave me strength and travelled with me in the journey of life. Whatever I am today, I owe a great deal to my revered mother, my teachers, my ever-supporting wife and the colleagues who shared my dreams and stood with me in hard times. My apologies to Surya Prakash for having tested his patience and wasted so much of his precious time which he could have well utilized for the benefit of his students and scholarship.

New Delhi
September, 2009

Prof. (Dr.) N.R. Madhava Menon

CONTENTS

Chapter I

In "God's Own Country"

IN "GOD'S OWN COUNTRY"

The princely State of Travancore in the Southern tip of India was a progressive kingdom in many respects. The Maharaja ruled his kingdom as an agent of Sri Padmanabha, the God who owned the land and its natural resources. The Sri Padmanabha temple is still the centre of attraction in the capital city of Thiruvananthapuram and all rulers of the erstwhile Travancore State governed as servants of the Lord, a trustee of its land and people. It is a beautiful concept in governance with important implications in law and administration.

There are legends and historical texts, which explain many customs and traditions followed by Travancoreans in those days. The onslaughts of conquerors and colonizers were not felt in that part of Bharatvarsha, which flourished in education and social reform movements much before they started elsewhere. Kerala's progress in education has its roots deep in the history of the land. In Travancore, the modern English education began even before the establishment of the three great universities *i.e.*, Madras, Bombay and Calcutta in early 1860's. The establishment of these universities had their impact on the princely State of Travancore. The Travancore and Cochin rulers (especially in Travancore under the Diwanship of T. Madhava Rao) granted liberal financial assistance even to private and missionary schools of foreign settlers and insisted that every school should be open to all. It was the beginning of universalization of primary education. Prof. John Galbrith has rightly remarked that in this world there is no literate population that is poor, no illiterate population other than poor. Today Kerala is the first totally literate State. In fact, literacy and development go together. There can be no progress without education for all.

I am lucky to be born in the peaceful, civilized city of Thiruvananthapuram on 4th May, 1935 when Europe was experiencing the dictatorship of Hitler and the rest of India was suffering under the yoke of British Colonial Rule. The Freedom Movement was picking up steam and Gandhiji became a household name everywhere in the country even though few in the south of the country had occasion to see or listen to him. No one could foresee clearly the developing political storm and the emerging clouds of Second World War. 1930s and 40s have been historically significant period for the whole world in general and India in particular; yet the average Travancoreans of those days seemed to have had little idea of the world outside and were immersed in life around the temple and the palace! Travancore was later merged with its northern neighbour of Kochi to make it Travancore-Cochin State. After the reorganization of States, in 1952 it assumed the name of Kerala, "God's own country"!

I belong to a "Marumakathayam" family where we inherit property from the maternal side and the maternal uncle is as important in the family affairs as the father. Though our original ancestral home is in Vaikom in central Travancore, my parents migrated to Thiruvananthapuram, in early 20th century where we had some family properties. My mother had her university education in Maharaja's college, Trivandrum. I was born to my parents as the fourth child in 1935 after three daughters Sukumari, Sarada and Sarojini. Naturally everyone in the family looked after me very well. As the first son in the family I enjoyed lots of love of my elders and attention of everyone around.

Difficulties in Childhood

I was named 'Appu' in my childhood. The "official" name given to me is a long one with the names of my maternal uncle (Neelakanta) followed by the name of my father (Ramakrishna) followed by the name of my grand father (Madhava) and ending with the surname of my father (Menon). Neelakanta Ramakrishna Madhava Menon was shortened as N.R. Madhava Menon or 'Appu' to elders in the family. My father Ramakrishna Menon after graduating with B.A. and B.L. joined the service with the Trivandrum Corporation as a Revenue Officer. The salary, my mother later told me, was around Rs. 60 per month which was quite sufficient for a small family in those days. Ambitious and industrious by nature, he had gone to Bombay for higher studies in municipal administration and had returned with another Diploma in the subject. Later, he had a promotion in his job. To pay homage to Lord Ayyappan, he made a pilgrimage to Sabarimalai, the hill temple of Kerala in 1937. When he returned after two weeks of arduous journey through thick forests and hills, he got an attack of typhoid while trekking the mountains in rains and cold. There was no effective treatment for typhoid at that time. He breathed his last when I was hardly two years old. My mother who was then only a house maker with no steady income except my father's salary was left helpless and with uncertain future. She was pregnant at the time of my father's death and it was an extremely hapless situation.

That was the time the Second World War was raging in Europe and India was being squeezed out of its resources by the colonial masters. Rice was in short supply and there was rationing for all essential commodities. People survived on Bajra, Tapioca or Ragi. Because of availability of limited food, my three elder sisters would have a portion of their food given to me in addition to my quota for keeping me in cheers and good health. All of us would watch other children dress up in new clothes for Onam, the greatest festival of Kerala and we had to be content with whatever our mother could organize out of her meagre income. Two of my younger brothers did not survive; the youngest died within two years and the elder who got a crippling disease, left studies and died later at the prime of youth leaving me as the only male member in the family. Along with other health problems they suffered malnutrition also. That life was indeed tough. It did make us realize that life is not all joy and God's grace is essential for survival.

After the demise of my father, my mother managed the family with the low wages she earned from her small job she secured in the Trivandrum Corporation. As father died while in service, the Corporation gave a clerical job to my mother on compassionate grounds. There were hardships throughout my education. My sisters voluntarily gave up many things they were entitled to so that I might get better nutrition and proper education. My mother, T.G. Bhavani Amma, had to manage the household, educate the five children and attend to her office work. My eldest sister Sukumari did her B.A. and B.Ed. and got a job as teacher in a government school. With her salary coming in, there was some relief in the family and hope of higher education for other children. My mother had seven sisters and a brother some of whom helped now and then in crisis situations.

Given the poor nutrition and conditions of life during those days, it was but natural that all of us needed medical help very often. One of the younger sisters of my mother, Dr. G. Kamalamma, then a doctor at Women's hospital at Thycaud (Trivandrum) used to treat us and gave medicines liberally without any cost. Occasionally my mother used to borrow money and provisions from her and other sisters as well. When things were too desperate my mother's sisters used to take us for short periods to their homes particularly during school vacations. My mother being the eldest of all the seven sisters, she used to command a lot of affection and respect which helped me and my sisters to grow up as children with many 'mothers' to look after.

My mother was a strict disciplinarian and none dared to cross the limits she prescribed in our activities. My school, Sree Moola Vilasom Government High School was located just opposite to the City

Corporation where my mother used to work as a clerk. My routine was to get ready at nine in the morning and accompany my mother to her office, wait by her side till the first bell rang and then rush to the school across the road for the morning prayers with my bag full of books. She would sometimes give a surprise visit to the school and consult my teachers about my studies, conduct and discipline. She would ask me to go to her office for meals at noon and report again soon after the final bell in the evening at 4 p.m. Between 4 p.m. and 5 p.m. I used to linger around the corporation building where my mother's colleagues would exchange pleasantries and report to mother if I ventured to get out on to the road. By 5 p.m. I would proceed with mother back to home where my three sisters would have returned from their school and begun cooking and other household chores. I would get an hour or so to play that too in and around the vicinity of home where I would be able to respond to a call from my mother or sisters.

Discipline was vigorous and any violation would attract severe punishment. Many times I had received beating from mother for either neglecting homework or for playing beyond the prescribed time and area. An old tennis ball was our football and it often went in all directions particularly when we had no play ground as such. I do not think I enjoyed my childhood in play and rejoicing as other children do. The love and affection liberally bestowed by my three elder sisters and the care and protection they provided more than compensated what I missed in fun and frolic.

Impressions on Independence Movement and School Education

I was hardly 12 years old at the time of Independence of the country. The princely state of Travancore was not a part of the Indian Union at that time. What I could understand from the events of the times was that the Maharaja was very much inclined to join with the Indian Union whereas the then Diwan of Travancore Sir C.P. Ramaswamy Iyer was hesitant to agree without conditions. The Indian National Congress had to motivate people to agitate against the Diwan. It was around that time the Punnapra-Vayalar communist struggle was also launched which was ruthlessly suppressed with police force by the Diwan. The net result was there were too many jathas and meetings during that period and people were agitated against Sir C.P. There was also mounting pressure to let the State join with the Indian Union. One evening there was a music festival in the Swati Tirunal Academy, Trivandrum and I was also listening to it outside the hall. Suddenly there was lot of commotion and I heard that somebody attacked Sir C.P. and part of his nose was chopped off. That was the incident, which triggered my enthusiasm to know more about freedom movement and the politics surrounding it. Later I learnt from unfolding events how the Congress and Pattom Thanu Pillai-led party and others forced the Diwan to flee Travancore and successfully completed the integration of Travancore with the rest of India.

I studied at SMV School, a leader in School Education in Trivandrum. I had very few friends at school. My friends had to be necessarily known and liked by my mother as well. I never had a girl friend while in school or in college. Talking to a girl was considered a taboo. All my teachers at school were also men and some of them were outstanding by all standards. I can never forget my English teacher George Sir, always cheerful, a hard task master and a man who conveyed the impression that there was nothing more important in the syllabus than English language. He used to ask the more enterprising amongst us in the class to consult the dictionary, select five new English words, spell them and explain it's meaning next day in the class. No doubt, it enriched our vocabulary and made us feel important enough to be recognized in a class of over sixty students.

Another teacher who impressed the children most was Shri M.P. Appan who taught us Mathematics. He looked an actor with flowing curly hair and spotless white Dhoti and Jubba. Later he became Poet Laureate (Mahakavi) of Kerala with many of his Malayalam poems winning State and National Awards. In those days, because of teachers of great reputation and commitment, SMV School was the most preferred school in the city. I felt proud to be a student of SMV where I studied from the preparatory class to the higher secondary class from 1940-1949. I was just an above average student and there are not many notable achievements in my school education. I liked English, Biology and Arithmetics and used to score better marks in those subjects. When I reached the Matriculation class (Xth Standard) I was one of the youngest in school (14 years) and I had to procure an exemption certificate for being below age to write the public examination.

Rich Cultural Traditions and Memorable Days of Family Reunion

India is rich in its diversity of cultures and traditions. Diversity is its virtue. Kerala too has its share of very rich traditions and endearing cultural manifestations. The childhood experience of several festivals celebrated during that period is still fresh in my memory. There has been the annual festival at our ancestral home in Maniyasseri, Vaikom that usually fell during the summer vacation. It was an occasion when all members of the "Maniyasseri Tarwad" joined together for about a week or more to worship the family deities with usual festivities including poojas and fireworks. The preparation for the festival rituals took a couple of months or more and the elders attended to it from their respective homes and villages. As the members of the family lived in different parts of Kerala and some outside the State, it was a great occasion of re-union long cherished by all, particularly children. Everyone young and old had a role in it and each one would do his or her best to excel in that role to receive blessings from our "Swami and other Devatas" as well as the family elders. As soon as the annual examinations were over we would work overtime to prepare ourselves in new bhajans and dances, dramas on divine themes etc. My interest was in Ottam Thullal (a type of folk dance) and Katha Prasangam (story telling interspersed with popular music and jokes) which I attempted sometimes in College festivals as well.

In a tributary of the Muvattupuzha river nearby the Maniyasseri Tarwad, we used to take bath and get ready for the poojas which began early morning. We spent hours together singing to please the Gods and Goddesses and to get their blessings. These annual festivities continue even now though there have been some changes in the scale of activities and the duration of the festivities. As one of the senior members of the Tarwad now, I took the lead to help raise a "Pooja Fund Trust" to look after the daily pooja needs of our ancestral home which is now known as Maniyasseri Temple of Gandharva Swami (the Presiding Deity of Maniyasseri).

What was most interesting for me to recollect is the journey from Trivandrum to Vaikom, a distance of 200 kms, which we used to complete in three days through multiple modes of transport. We used to take the train from Trivandrum to Quilon (65 kms), which took nearly six to eight hours or more with inevitable stops and crossings in intermittent stations. From Quilon railway station to boat jetty was a long stretch of walking with luggage on our shoulders and hands. The journey from Quilon to Alleppy (90 kms) used to be negotiated by boat fitted with diesel engines which used to collect passengers and goods from both sides of the rivers, canals and backwaters. On an average it took 20 to 28 hours to reach Alleppy. When the boat stopped at an important town we used to go out to eat and collect things for our consumption in the rest of the journey. Some vendors used to rush into the boat with their wares making a lot of noise and fun. The scenic beauty of backwaters, with enthralling coconut grooves the entire journey was exhilarating particularly for children. From Alleppy we used to take another boat along the Vembanad Lake to reach Vaikom in about 8 to 10 hours. From Vaikom we used to get into yet another non-mechanized vallom (boat) sent by my maternal uncle with two of his trusted workers. The journey was very slow but extremely enjoyable particularly if it happened to be a moonlit night. Sometimes we took bus journey (if we were lucky to get one) from Vaikom to Toll Junction a distance of six kilometers. Today most of the members of the family have their cars and cover the whole distance from Trivandrum in 3 to 4 hours; but they are missing the joy of leisurely travel through multiple modes of transport. My grand children cannot even believe when I say that I had traveled in steam-driven, both sides open buses which used to stop every 20 kms to put more coal and water to propel the bus for a further 20 kms.

In my youth, I was very much influenced by the personality of Swami Vivekananda. In my early days of school life I had heard and read about him. I am not a deeply religious person, but I am not an atheist. I was introduced by mother and sisters to religious rituals and worshipping of family deity and the Goddess of Chettikulangara Temple near my home. Every house in those days used to have a puja room where in the evenings there was formal lighting of oil lamps after which all children would have to assemble and recite certain religious slokas and devotional songs. Elders used to read the scriptures like Ramayana, Bhagavatam and Gita. While my sisters knew many songs by heart and recited them in unison, I would sit with folded hands as if in transcendence. It went on for an hour and half and unless this exercise is completed every evening, the dinner would not be served. I felt the serenity of chanting the religious scriptures which I was told would purify the atmosphere and enliven the mind and the soul. It was a sort of rigorous discipline that was cultivated to influence the young children to be God-fearing and religious. No doubt, it had a lasting influence in shaping my thoughts about my Creator, my parents and the whole universe of which I am just a speck endowed with duties to perform and life to serve.

Introduction to Religion and Spirituality

My mother while working in the Trivandrum Corporation used to conduct Gita classes at our home in Vanchiyoor and the children from neighbourhood were called to listen to discourses on Gita. Probably this gave her solace and peace of mind in the hard days. It used to be on Sunday afternoons for about three to four hours. Mother used to study and prepare herself the meanings of various verses, consulting the Sanskrit-English dictionary and interpretations of various scholars. She then used her own language and interpretted the slokas (couplets in Sanskrit from ancient texts) through stories so that children could understand the essence of the message. When this became a regular feature in our home, it attracted children from several relatives' families who offered to feed children with snacks and sweets. The main attraction of some of us was the refreshment that came to be distributed at the end of the Gita class. Some well-to-do families used to bring some delicious sweets and fruits which were distributed to the children to make them listen to my mother's religious instructions in the class. In fact, my mother's Doctor sister gave funds to construct a permanent pandal in front of our house at Vanchiyoor exclusively for the Gita Class. This memorable community service continued till my mother became seriously ill in mid 1970s. She had become a "Guru" to many children in the extended family in Vanchiyoor and connected places in Trivandrum.

The concept of God which I learnt from my mother is to be faithful in your thoughts and actions and always trying to be helpful to others. She told us, in doing so, you would yourself be really benefitted in life. Some supernatural force, which dwells in us as well as in all living creatures, usually called God Almighty manifests in everyone's life on occasions where one feels helpless and deserted. If one cultivates such friendly and noble feeling, one will be different in thoughts, in actions, in attitudes and will have peace with life around. That sort of feeling to my mind is Godliness or Spirituality. In one sense it is compatible with Adhvaita of Sri Shankaracharya. When you consider that you are yourself "Viswatma" or part of the cosmic consciousness, you will conclude that God is ubiquitous and omnipresent. It is only to train and tune the mind to feel Him in real life and to understand Him that one needs religion in the spiritual sense. That does not mean that one can disregard the rituals and visual forms of Gods and Goddesses. Hinduism comprises of a variety of rituals and diverse philosophies while propounding the underlying truth of 'one ness'. You can be an atheist and still be a Hindu. That sort of broadness in religion accommodating all conflicts in thoughts and practices into a commitment for broader human values is the greatness of Hindu religion. In fact, Hinduism is a way of living. The art of living with Nature with all its diversities is inherent in Hinduism as I perceive it.

In the year 1954 I was blessed by a spiritual 'Guru'. I was then just 19 studying law in Ernakulam. During the summer vacation, I got an opportunity to accompany my mother's younger sister, a Civil Surgeon in Dhangadra in Gujarat and an ardent devotee of Swami Madhava Tirth of Sabarmati in Ahmedabad. Attending for over a month her two-hour-long daily poojas at home, I picked up some of the Mantras and an urge to understand something about our heritage beyond the rituals. Guru poornima approached and we proceeded to Ahmedabad to pay respects to her Guru Swami Madhava Tirth. A sprawling Ashram on the banks of the Sabarmati river, the Ashram had poojas and bhajans round the clock and devotees from all parts of India came and lived there as if it was their ancestral home. The same evening I participated in a Grand Bhajan where I saw that saintly figure, the Head of the Ashram, Swami Madhava Tirth, a highly educated Gujarati giving everybody spiritual bliss and religious education. At the end of his discourse, there was "Aarti" with an emotionally-surcharged prayer reverberating the whole place and making devotees forget all other thoughts and worries.

A little later, my "Kochamma", (Mother's younger sister) Dr. G. Rudrani Amma, took me to Swamiji and introduced me to him. He asked few questions about my study and future plans and directed me to see him at his abode an hour later. Apparently my Kochamma had requested Swamiji much earlier to bless me with "Diksha" and induct me to the Spiritual Universe even though I was too young to go spiritual. As expected, when I went to him later, he had decided to take me as his disciple. He gave me that "Divine Mantra" which I chant eversince. It gives me a rare sense of security and a mental strength to withstand difficult circumstances. Swamiji left the material world some years later. My Kochamma also died. But both of them live in my mind constantly guiding me with their blessings and to be always God-fearing, righteous and compassionate.

Rarely does one get a chance to have a Spiritual Guru early in life. I got it because it was the wish of my beloved mother who had entrusted the job to her younger sister. Spirituality is much more than religiousness. It is the beauty of ancient Indian philosophy that it preaches spiritual education side by side with material acquisition of knowledge. This is what Swami Vivekananda called "education which brings out what is best in Man, which is latent in every individual."

Unguided Transition to Higher Education

I passed my Higher Secondary or Matriculation examination in the year 1949. From that year the State changed over from the then existing two-year intermediate programme to a one year pre-university course (PUC) and a three-year Degree course. I was in the first batch of PUC which got started in Kerala in 1949-50. After completing PUC, there were many options to join in B.A./B.Com./B.Sc. or go for professional degrees. So, after one year PUC I joined the B.Sc. Degree programme with Zoology as main subject and botany and chemistry as ancillary subjects. I completed my B.Sc. degree from S.D. College, Alleppy. At that time my mother was particular that I should become a doctor.

However, circumstances willed otherwise and I became a lawyer! When I graduated in 1953, a medical college was started in Trivandrum. Though I sought a seat in the very first batch I was not lucky to get admitted. My mother desired to send me for medical education outside the State; but economic compulsions did not permit my seeking admission outside Trivandrum. The option was either to go for an M.Sc. Programme or do some professional course. There was nobody to guide or advise in this regard. My mother was not able to decide as to which course other than medicine would be appropriate for my future. She used to ask her colleagues and some of them suggested that law or English literature would be suitable for me. So, the options available were to become a teacher, a lawyer, a scientist or a civil servant. Ultimately it was concluded that a law career would be good since there was a law college in Trivandrum to which I could go from my home daily. It was economically also a more viable option for me.

'Man proposes and God disposes' is a trite saying. To our utter disappointment, the Government of the day decided to shift the Trivandrum law college to Ernakulam as part of a political settlement with the State of Cochin which merged with Travancore to form the State of Travancore-Cochin. The seat of the High Court also got shifted to Cochin. So, when finally I made up my mind to join law, the law college got shifted to Ernakulam. Again, it created many problems for my mother. She had to find a place for me to live in Ernakulam to be able to study law. She was not at all willing to admit me either in the hostel, or for my discontinuation from law studies. My mother searched for all available options and ultimately found that one of my grandfather's brother was living in Ernakulam. She along with her brother (my maternal uncle) went and requested him to accommodate me for some time in his place. He gave me his out-house, a one room facility, where I used to stay and walk down the distance of 3 kms., to the law college at Ernakulam. The walk was very pleasant as it was through the busy Ernakulam town full of shops and educational institutions. The Law College was just opposite to the boat jetty in the Cochin Assembly building. There was St. Theresa College for Women next to our college. The law college students used to give whistles and constant headache to the Theresa hostel residents. Some of them were very notorious for mischief and eve-teasing. The people were disgusted with the law college students mainly coming from Travancore region. Astonishingly some of the seniors used to cross the ferry to go to the nearby island in the Arabian Sea to have a taste of the local toddy and come back to the classes drunk! Students' Union politics kept the leaders busy for half the year and classes were neglected. Students in city colleges feared the law college crowd who were considered politicians in the making. Occasional lectures in the college of some eminent advocates on sensational cases inspired some of us to learn the skills of advocacy through debate and mooting.

The stay at Ernakulam brought new wings of freedom for me. I learnt to manage on my own largely free from the regimental discipline of my mother. I was conscious of the fact that I was being educated at great cost and sacrifice on the part of my mother and sisters. I felt responsibility for the first time in my life and realized that I had to show good results and progress. I became conscious of the harsh realities of life. The regimen under which I was brought up would not allow me to deviate from the right path. Even going to the cinema house was taboo. Letters from my mother constantly reminded me of my responsibilities and the need to strive towards excellence to achieve the goal. A year quickly passed and I successfully completed what used to be called F.L. or the first year in law with good academic grades. As luck would have it, the Government decided to shift the law college back to Trivandrum and allowed the Ernakulam one to continue as a new college affiliated to another University. My second year in law (B.L.) was spent in Trivandrum Law College located close to my home. I took some interest in the Student Union activities and got elected as the Editor of the Law College Magazine. I put the opportunity to good use, became a small leader in college and mobilized students to work with me for producing the first Law College Magazine carrying a number of articles on legal subjects. Dr. A.T. Markose a well-known teacher in Administrative Law was my Staff Advisor in College Magazine production. He was very kind to me and later persuaded me to take an academic career. It is on his advice I took to research and later full-time teaching assignment at Aligarh Muslim University. By that time he also moved to Delhi as the first Director of the Indian Law Institute.

Many of my classmates, who were very bright and successful, later joined the Secretariat of the Accountant General's office which was supposed to be very good as it carried the highest starting salary those days (Rs. 600 per month) outside the Central Civil Services (IAS). I was also tempted; but my mother on the advice of all elders in the family asked me to join the bar and practice law. Her idea was to see me as a judge eventually. According to her reading of my horoscope, that was what astrologers found in it!

Looking back to my days in the Law College, I am myself surprised as to how I suddenly joined student politics, contested elections and won a place in the College Union. Of course, it was a minor office; yet for a person with my background it was a big boost to find one's name flashed in posters and published in newspapers. I used to write letters to the Editor in The Hindu and some were published. In those days to get a letter published in "The Hindu" was considered to be an accomplishment for a student. That perhaps projected me as a possible candidate for the college magazine. So, I was put up as a candidate for editorship of the law college magazine, which kept me busy in a variety of related activities. I totally concentrated on producing a good journal at the end of my student career at law college, Trivandrum. I completed the assignment successfully. I used to meet and collect notes and articles from different reputed lawyers and judges in the city and used to discuss with them various legal issues. The process of editing student articles in consultation with an eminent jurist like Dr. A.T. Markose taught me a lot. Previously I had no concept of how to write case comments; nevertheless I picked up some elementary things in legal writing and legal research from Prof. Markose and some other teachers like Mr. S. Easwara Iyer and Mr. V.P. Pillai. When I had time, I assiduously went about collecting a lot of photographs of great lawyers, jokes about lawyers etc. I never failed in any class during my entire academic career but I have not been able to get the top ranks in any of my examinations. The first notable performance in my education was what I made in my editorial foray in the Trivandrum law college magazine. To find some advertisements to cover extra costs and to get the journal printed was indeed a great challenge as I was new to the job. It was a memorable experience and this venture inculcated in me some writing and publication interests. Still I preserve a copy of the magazine as a memento of an "elected editor who never before wrote an article for public consumption!".

At that time Prof. M. George was our principal. He had his higher education in U.S.A. and his command over the language and law was appreciated by all. His wife, also American educated, was a Professor of Home Science in Women's college, Trivandrum. Prof. George used to teach us Roman law, a subject nobody liked and nobody failed. One used to study few topics by heart and had to reproduce it in the examinations without understanding its content or meaning! Prof. George used to give different kinds of questions including the fill-up the blanks type. Students used to get 80% to 90% of marks in that subject. Today Roman Law is taken out of the LL.B. curriculum, making law students lament the disappearance of the only opportunity they had to score like mathematics in law studies.

First Steps in the Legal Profession

I completed my law at a very young age, just when I was completing my 19th year. In fact, I had to get special permission from Government to appear in B.L. examination. Again it was Prof. Markose who pursued my case with the authorities to get the exemption needed. I successfully completed my B.L. in 1955 and got into a thirteen month apprenticeship with a well known senior Advocate Mr. V. Nagappan Nair whose office was located next to my house in Vanchiyoor. In 1956 I became an Advocate, admitted to the Kerala High Court at Cochin. Next year and a half I practiced as an Advocate, mostly on the criminal side in the District Court of Trivandrum. My senior was Poovanpallil Neelakanta Pillai who was related to me as he was my mother's sister's husband.

For me the struggle to earn a living had started. My mother used to say that as an advocate, I was expected to earn something for covering my personal needs. But who would give cases to a fresh advocate. How could I ask for money from my senior particularly when he was not convinced of my abilities as a lawyer. Many in the office including clients of my senior did not even recognize me as an Advocate despite my black coat and gown! I was afraid of the judge who was an imposing figure managing the court in monosyllables.

The day when I put on the full uniform of an advocate a sparkle flashed in the eyes of my mother. It was a proud moment for her and the rest of the family. We went to the studio for a group photograph, all of us in convocation robes. People may laugh now, if I say that it was the first occasion I wore a shoe. It was a necessary part of the apparel of an Advocate and I found myself the proud owner of a pair of Bata shoes. I had neither shoes nor chappals till I became a lawyer no matter what the season might be. We used to walk barefoot during school and college days. Then it was a problem to wear shoes. My feet which enjoyed liberty since birth did not fit into standard size ordinary shoes. I needed a special size that was not usually available in the market. I felt uncomfortable to remain in the shoes throughout the court time. I used to take out the shoe and my seniors used to rebuke me for that. Slowly and steadily I got used to remain with the shoes the whole day!

My senior had good number of sessions' cases and in some matters I also appeared with him and that developed interest in me in criminal law. When he won a murder case as a defense lawyer, the news came in the city newspapers. It was a serious murder trial and the accused got acquitted. The newspapers reported that Sri Neelakantha Pillai and

Sri Madhava Menon as an assisting lawyer argued the case. Oh! What a joy? I took the clipping of the paper and showed it to my mother which she circulated among her sisters and other visitors to our home. As an assisting lawyer, I used to do research on precedents with Law Reports and accompanied my senior to court. I was not comfortable in the Bar Association Hall and avoided other Advocates who put uncomfortable questions. Some of the clients when they won the cases used to distribute money among the clerks of the senior and occasionally gave me also something. However, senior clerks were paid more than the junior lawyers.

At that time, I was searching other avenues to earn some money. Accidentally it happened that one of my mother's sister who was a doctor happened to have a senior official of the All India Radio visiting her for medical consultation. Once when I visited her I was introduced to this official. She asked him if he could help me in doing some part time work in AIR programmes without prejudice to my profession. There was some procedure for selection to participate in the programmes of AIR. So, he asked me to attend a voice test in the studios which I promptly did in a couple of days and I passed it. So, I became a part-time artiste of AIR Station, Trivandrum. They used to call me for rehearsal now and then and recording of the plays to be broadcast through the AIR. For a job of half an hour or 45 minutes they used to pay me Rs. 50 or Rs. 80. I used to get occasional programmes which brought some money which I could not earn in my legal profession. I also started writing articles in the newspapers that also gave me some income though not much. I used to do all sundry jobs including teaching tutorial classes along with my profession for nearly one and half years. That was the beginning and end of my glorious days as a practicing Advocate at the Trivandrum Bar!

Chapter II

Migration to Delhi: In Search of a Career

MIGRATION TO DELHI: IN SEARCH OF A CAREER

I was not very comfortable with my status as a junior lawyer depending on financial support from home and was looking for an opportunity to do something challenging outside legal practice. My inclination was for higher studies in law for which there was no opportunity in Trivandrum. I wrote the Civil Services Examination and was called for the interview, but failed to get the rank desired for selection. I was assigned the Central Secretariat Service for which my mother was not willing to send me all the way to Delhi.

The year was 1957. My teacher at the Law College, Trivandrum Prof. A.T. Markose took an assignment as the first Director of the newly established Indian Law Institute and moved to New Delhi. I met him during one of his visits to his home at Ernakulam and sought his advice on what I should be doing for my career. His considered opinion was that I should go for higher studies in law and take an academic career. I told him about my financial difficulties and the reluctance on the part of my mother to let me go to a far away place without steady income. I had never travelled alone nor had I gone outside Kerala till then. Dr. Markose was of the opinion that Delhi offered facilities to pursue higher studies while working and I should therefore take up the Central Government job at least till I completed my higher studies in law to make myself eligible for a teaching position in a University. He persuaded my mother accordingly and I left for the unknown land, the Nation's Capital, 2500 kilometers away. What I knew about Delhi was from history books, the city built by the Mughals and colonized by the British and where Mahatma Gandhi was murdered by his own countrymen!

The train journey in a third class compartment for four days (between Trivandrum and Delhi) without any sleeping facility or proper food was horrible though I did not feel so at that time. I had to first go by meter gauge train from Trivandrum to Madras which took one and half days. From Madras Egmore Station one had to go to Madras Central Station to catch the Grand Trunk Express, the only train available to Delhi which was always crowded with passengers and goods. It was indeed an adventure which I hardly enjoyed. My mother had packed Idlies and Chutney for my entire journey and had instructed me not to get down from the train unless there was a long stoppage in a big station. She had also asked one or two co-passengers from Trivandrum to help me out in case of any difficulty. My plus point was my advanced learning of Hindi for a diploma "Visharad" from the Dakshin Bharat Hindi Prachar Sabha, Madras (now Chennai). Alas, on the fifth day I reached the Delhi Railway Station, tired and hungry not knowing my fate in coming days. My Sanskritised Hindi made people laugh in Delhi and dismiss me as a "Madrasi", a generic contemptuous expression for rice-eating, timid South-Indians ! Thanks to the intense search of a Delhi-based contact person which my mother and sisters did for several weeks before my departure, they could locate a distant relative from Kerala (whose name I am unable to recollect) and had sought his assistance for my initial stay in the capital. He was a Stenographer living alone in a room sub-let by another government servant in a place called Lodhi Colony. To my great relief he located me at the railway platform and took me to his room for temporary stay till alternate accommodation was found. There was one Nair's restaurant at the corner of the main street in Lodhi Road where South-Indian employees assembled twice every day, once in the morning for a full meal and the other in the evening for dinner or snacks. I also joined the group and soon got used to the style of daily routine of office work, occasional Malayalam cinema at Connaught Place and rest in the shared accommodation. I got along well with my host that we decided to share the rent and save money instead of paying extra amount for another room because we needed accommodation only for sleeping in the night.

Early Days in Delhi

I joined government service and earned a princely sum of Rs. 480 per month of which Rs. 150 was sent to my mother in Trivandrum. Sometimes when I had to meet some extra expenditure I used to ask her and received more money from her than I had sent her before. I bought a cycle, joined the M.A. course in the Campus College of Punjab University at Gole Market and became extremely busy with office work and pursuit of scholarship. To avoid cycling long distances in busy Delhi roads, I moved to Karol Bagh to live with another friend, Mr. Sadanandan who had two-bed room flat which provided some exclusive space for my study as well. I passed M.A. degree examination with distinction in Political Science. Professor Markose soon got me a teaching-cum-research assistantship at Aligarh Muslim University to let me take up an academic career in the Law Faculty there. I resigned my government job in Delhi and moved to Aligarh in 1959, within two years of my coming to Delhi. Thus began a journey which put me on a career I was looking forward to ever since I completed my B.L. Degree at Trivandrum.

In Indian tradition a 'Guru' is more than a Teacher. The first twenty years of my life was spent under the care and protection of my mother and three elder sisters who shaped my personality as a God-fearing, rather timid, family-centred youth. In the law college, Dr. A.T. Markose was my favourite Professor who turned out to be a godfather to me in shaping my later career. What endeared him to me was his profound scholarship, his devotion to legal education and legal research and his willingness to work for the welfare of his students.

Prof. Markose was the Staff Advisor when I worked as the elected student editor of the Trivandrum Law College Magazine during 1954-'55. He got to know me as a person and started liking me. Always, he advised me to pursue higher studies in law and consider taking up an academic career. To my pleasant surprise, Prof. Markose moved to Delhi to take up the assignment of Directorship of the Indian Law Institute. When I met him in Delhi he asked me whether I was prepared to move to Aligarh to pursue higher studies in law if a scholarship was given by the University. I consulted my mother and sisters who believed that whatever my teacher advised would be in my best interest. I resigned the job in Delhi and joined the Faculty of Law, Aligarh Muslim University from where I completed my LL.M. with distinction in all subjects and took up my first job there. The Dean at Aligarh, Prof. Hafeez-ul-Rehman, a towering personality and a keen observer of men and matters was a good friend of Dr. A.T. Markose. The two together took care of my induction to the academic world in which I lived with a sense of fulfillment for the next fifty years!

By the time I shifted to Delhi University in 1965, Dr. Markose had left Law Institute and had returned to Kerala. In the next few years he took active interest in two Committees on re-organizing legal education in the State headed by retired Chief Justice B.P. Sinha and himself as Member-Secretary. He started an independent Post-Graduate Law Department in the University of Kerala at Cochin which later became part of Cochin University. During that period he visited Delhi and did not forget to call on me. I was at that time having additional charge of Wardenship of Jubilee Hall in Delhi University and was living in an isolated house on the Ridge amidst Nature's bounty. He visited my home and had food with us. He always liked papaya and green chillies and asked me to arrange for it too. It was a pleasure to see him eat the two while giving us a lecture of their medicinal qualities.

Dr. Markose was a jovial man who would make others also see the joy of life while in his company. He would not tolerate mediocrity and would not hesitate to call a spade a spade irrespective of whether the person involved is a judge or a Minister. He might have paid the price for being too independent in a society which institutionalized sychophancy and hero worship. Whenever I remember Dr. Markose, what comes to my mind is his love for Malayalam literature, Hindu epics and Kathakali about which he would keep me engaged for hours together. After my marriage, both of us went to him to seek his blessings. I thought he would give me a chance to work under him in Kerala. Instead he asked me to continue to serve outside the State, learn more and satisfy desires in life before thinking of returning to the State. In retrospect, I see it as a sound piece of advice. Had I joined him as a Lecturer in Kerala, I would have at best become a Professor and retired without having the many academic adventures I had in institution building and comparative scholarship in diverse environments.

Dr. Markose used to track my progress and say good things about me to mutual acquaintances. When I was serving as Principal of Government Law College, Pondicherry he telephoned me to seek my help in accommodating his daughter who was then seeking admission to the Medical College there. I did it with pleasure for which he thanked me. Few years later, I heard of his sudden demise after cardiac arrest in London where he had gone on a British Council Fellowship to research on the final years of the Privy Council jurisdiction over India. I was sad to read in newspapers that it took several days for the body to be brought to India because of some technical reasons. I went later to pay my respects and share the grief with the family of the deceased. I continue to feel that Dr. Markose, who wrote the first book on Judicial Control of Administrative Action and took a lead role in setting up the Indian Law Institute did not get the recognition he deserved. He should have been a judge of the Supreme Court and this view was held by many even during his life time. I pay my humble tributes to my teacher who in different ways influenced me to take an academic career and guided me in the formative years of my life.

Memorable Years at Aligarh

The scholarship and training at Aligarh Muslim University shaped my career which I continued even after I left with LL.M. and Ph.D. degrees. I spent almost six years at AMU as a teacher and researcher in Law. In those days Aligrah was a small University town known (in a lighter vein) for three Ms – Muslim, Makhan and Macher (Mosquitoes). Makhan stood for "buttering", an art everyone should learn to advance and enjoy campus life with full privileges. The game was highly competitive and involved risks at times. The University in those days was a unique place for learning and living. The teacher-student relationship was excellent and everybody took the same food ("Dunlop" as the roti was known) irrespective of whether one was a teacher, student or employee. Sir Syed Ahmed Khan Dinner in October every year was indeed a great event to cherish. The University song was inspiring and memorable. The campus was full of life all the time. And the monthly expense was a princely sum of Rs. 150, of which 25 rupees towards room rent, 60 rupees for mess charges and the rest towards tuition fees and sundry charges ! There was no way to spend money even if one was inclined and resourceful excepting when the renowned "namayiz" (exhibition) came to the city once every year.

I passed my LL.M. with distinction marks in all subjects and won the University Gold Medal. I was inducted into the administration by designating me as the resident warden in a group of dormitories at Sir Syed Hall. I was awarded a University Grants Commission Research Fellowship and got registered for the Ph.D. Degree along with teaching LL.B. classes. I was elected President of the AMU Malayalee Association, Vice-Captain of the AMU Horse-riding Club which were my other assignments during the period. I enjoyed teaching and learnt how to become a professional liked by students, colleagues and staff. I was appointed a full-fledged Lecturer in the Law Faculty of AMU thereby increasing my income and status. Things appeared set for a long innings at AMU when suddenly something unexpected happened. The then Vice Chancellor was Mr. Ali Yavar Jung who was not so popular with students for some unknown reasons. One day in 1965 during the meeting of the University Executive Council a section of students grew violent, assaulted him and few other members and dragged him through the Sir Syed Hall hostel. He was bleeding profusely and some persons pleaded with the students and got him released pushing him into one of the rooms of the hostel of which I was the Warden. The Central and State Governments got into action, the army moved in and occupied the Campus, University was closed and students were asked to vacate the halls of residence. By evening, among many others, over a dozen students of my hostel got arrested in my presence and I became a witness for the prosecution to give evidence against my own wards. The violent episode left an indelible impression on me, upset my plans of settling down at Aligarh and disturbed me for a long time to come.

"Hafeez Sab", was a master craftsman who shaped my career at Aligarh Muslim University. Prof. Hafeez-ul-Rehman under whom I worked at the instance of Dr. A.T. Markose between 1960 and 1965 was a different personality both as a teacher and colleague. A tall man with a sherwani and cap, "Hafeez Sab" was a terror to everybody in the Department. He looked grim all the time and murmured few words. It was difficult to know his mind and we (his students and fellow teachers) used to wait for hours together to have a meeting with him, sometimes unsuccessfully. When I passed LL.M. in first division with distinction in all subjects, he called me to know whether I would seek a Lecturership or join Ph.D. programme with U.G.C. Fellowship. He had meanwhile talked to Dr. Markose who, having got to know the mind of his friend, advised me to go for full-time research for Ph.D. and avoid applying for Lecturership for which advertisement was then issued by the University. I was taken aback on the advice; but, I had no choice in the circumstance. Hafeez Sab cleverly gave it an appearance that it was my own decision! He told me later in confidence that he would see my appointment as a Professor once I secured the degree of Ph.D. in Law.

Hafeez Sab was my Ph.D. guide and I was the first scholar under him to pursue Ph.D. with U.G.C. Scholarship. The subject I chose for study was "White Collar Crime" with focus on corruption and corporate fraud. To make my stay in Aligarh comfortable, Hafeez Sab got me appointed as Warden in Sir Syed Hall where the Law Faculty was then located. He wanted me to take classes as well which I did with lot of preparation and diligence. In due course he appointed me as a Lecturer while pursuing the doctoral studies.

Getting the draft thesis read and approved by him was a difficult task. I had to accompany him in some of his official tours and visit him at his house without being sure of being called. During this period, there was an All India Law Teachers' Conference in Kerala which Hafeez Sab decided to participate. He was visiting Kerala for the first time and wanted me to organize the visit. I did it with pleasure and took him for a treat at my Uncle's house in Eramalloor. My uncle who was a lawyer himself engaged him in conversation and took him on a boat ride through the backwaters of Central Tranvancore which he enjoyed thoroughly.

Hafeez Sab was a highly influential man not only in University affairs but also in several other circles. Looking at his capacity to manage difficult and complex situations and the way he kept all types of characters around him in tenterhooks, I often wondered why he did not take a role in national politics. He would have been a successful Minister in the State or Central Government. It is indeed remarkable of him that he got me selected as a Professor in 1968 at AMU immediately after my securing the Ph.D. degree. A promise made eight years ago got fulfilled. Though I could not take up the position, the fact that a young lecturer with less than eight years' experience could get selected directly to Professorship in a Central University boosted my morale and self-image. Thanks to Hafeez Sab who kept his promise when he asked me to join full-time research instead of going for Lecturership at a time when everyone in my position would have liked a secured job with higher income and status. This was Hafeez Sab, the master craftsman!

Years later I was invited to deliver the first Hafeez-ul-Rehman Memorial Lecture at Aligarh Muslim University. I considered it as an honour and spoke on Criminal Justice, a subject on which he was an expert. I recalled my tutelage under Hafeez Saheb and the many good things he had done to shape my career. What I acquired in Aligarh indeed built the foundation of my career as an academic and much of it I owe to Hafeez Sab, the man about whom I still know very little!

Marriage and a Disappointing Start of Family Life

Meanwhile my mother and sisters were planning my marriage ever since I got a regular teaching job at Aligarh Muslim University. I postponed the marriage on the grounds that I was pre-occupied with teaching, research and administration and would not get leave even for marriage. However, destiny decided otherwise. Soon after the tragic events of 1965, I proceeded on leave to Trivandrum and tied the nuptial knot on 8th July, 1965. It was an arranged marriage. The bride was none other than my maternal uncle's daughter who was identified for the purpose right from her birth without her knowing anything about it. I had some idea because in family circles I was often teased whenever I was found in her company. Rema Devi daughter of M. Neelakanta Kartha and Devaki Amma was at that time a second year B.Sc. student in Women's College, Trivandrum. The marriage was in two parts. The informal ceremony was in our Tarwad at Maniyasseri in the presence of family deities and the formal one a few days later at Trivandrum. After completion of the ceremonies, I rushed to Aligarh as I was summoned by the University authorities to give evidence in the police cases involving the assault on the Vice Chancellor. I had neither honeymoon nor could I convince my wife that my sudden departure was unavoidable. I could not bring her to Aligarh for obvious reasons. All this left a bad taste in married life at the beginning itself which I could not outlive for long. At Aligarh I felt lonely and sad but got reconciled to my fate. I badly needed a change which came within a couple of months rather unexpectedly. I got appointed as a lecturer in the Law Faculty of Delhi University for which I had applied few months earlier. A God sent opportunity and a welcome change from the depressing atmosphere of post-riot Aligarh. I joined Delhi University on 26th August, 1965.

Besides my mother who had been a source of strength for me, the one other person who shared all my worries and set backs and steered the way forward is my life partner for 45 years, Mrs. Rema Devi. She has many things to complain; but seldom does. With infinite patience and quite sufferance she confronts life's problems, saying that God will not let her down when all humans do, the same attitude which my mother entertained in her life. Few incidents illustrate her personality as much as they do of mine.

Soon after marriage in 1965 I had to rush to Aligarh for some official work leaving her in Trivandrum where she continued studies. I could not realize how painful it was for a woman who dreamt of honeymoon and all the rest. Nor did she convey her feelings at that time to me. Probably people at home also did not understand her agony and she had to suffer occasional taunts without her being able to share them with me. I was so pre-occupied with my official responsibilities at Aligarh Muslim University and my change to Delhi University that I could not reflect on the sense and sensibilities of my spouse, which it was my duty upon marriage. Years later she did narrate her sufferings of that period and reminded me of my "cruelty", though unintended. I realized counseling in marriage is necessary if the foundation is to be strong and mutually supportive. I tried to make amends though not very successfully. Perhaps some wounds are expected to remain so long as one lives.

Having lost my father at the age of two, I owe everything to my mother who with a small income from a job in the City Corporation and very little support from family sources, educated her five children and maintained the home in adverse circumstances. Her absolute faith in God and determination to struggle for the welfare of her children are characteristic of Indian womanhood in its sublime sense. I believe that mother's blessings will bring success in unexpected ways. Few reminiscences which reveal her unbounded love and affection for me can be recalled as they are fresh in my memory.

Memories of Mother's Love Unqualified

I was leaving for Delhi looking for a better career and seeking higher studies in law. For days together she looked worried and was consulting astrologers on my future. She went about arranging all sorts of poojas in every other temple in Trivandrum taking me along. She asked elders in the family and outside to advise me how to behave and organize life when I was in the alien environment in Delhi. She herself wrote down my daily routine and instructed me what to eat and what to avoid. After a great deal of effort she could locate someone distantly related in Delhi who was persuaded to take care of me on reaching there. Having heard of Delhi weather, she was assembling some woollen clothing, difficult to get in Trivandrum in those days. And finally when the day of departure arrived, she was literally in tears and along with my sisters and younger brother accompanied me to the railway station where she was found seeking the help of every other passenger travelling to Delhi to take care of me. I felt a little embarrassed to tell my co-passengers that I am an Advocate and was going to Delhi to take up a job in the Government of India. They wondered why my mother and sisters were so upset that they treated me as a child who would not be able to manage the journey without help. Few of my friends who had also come to the station were found consoling my mother and taking her away as the train started moving out of the station. There is no one in the world to whom every person owes so much in life as one's mother; and those who do not respect motherhood can achieve nothing in life. She is the embodiment of nobility, sacrifice and true love.

Another episode later in life which I would like to recall happened when my mother came to live for few days with me in Delhi. I was still a lecturer drawing less then Rs. 800 a month living with family in the quarters of the Warden of Jubilee Hall. I had promised that I would take her to all the religious places in North India which she had been talking about for long. We first went to Hardwar and Rishikesh. She enjoyed the pilgrimage as it was a short trip from Delhi. Next we travelled to Triveni Sangam, the confluence of the three rivers the Ganga, Yamuna and the mystic Saraswati in Allahabad where she was keen to perform the rituals we do for departed souls. The boat ride was rather stressful because of the continuing and quarrelsome bargains between the boatmen and the pundits amidst which we were made to pay not only a lot of money but also our clothes! I wanted to protest and challenge them but my mother would not let me do anything like that. She saw in everything God's hand and she was prepared for any hardship or sacrifice. She believed in all the rituals particularly those associated with what Hindu Dharma prescribed in relation to the deceased. The annual "Shraddha" ceremony of my father was one event which she got solemnized religiously by all her children. And she considered it her good fortune that she could get that performed in her lifetime at the most sacred of all places, namely "Triveni". The visit to Varanasi also known as Kashi and Benaras was a memorable experience. The city is one of the oldest in Indian history and is believed to be the place of unbroken habitation for 5000 years. Mark Twain once wrote that Benaras is older than history, older than tradition, older even than legend and looks twice as old as all of them put together. All Hindus, piligrims or travellers, sadhus and saints are irresistibly drawn to Varanasi. The finest temples and most importantly the temple of Lord Viswanath is the main attraction in the city. The great evening Arati is a crowd puller on the banks of holy river Ganga which is conducted from times immemorial. To complete the pilgrimage at Varanasi with another ritual on the banks of Ganga together with visit to the famous temples of Benares was indeed a satisfying experience to all of us. Before she travelled back to Trivandrum I took her to Mathura-Vrindavan also which she thoroughly enjoyed. My mother recorded her experiences in her diary and conveyed excerpts to me which I still preserve as valuable assets in my personal possession.

I became an Author and a Noted Teacher

As luck would have it, within two years of my joining Delhi University I was appointed Warden of Jubilee Hall with a small but decent accommodation on the edge of the Ridge with peacocks and monkeys for company. My wife completed her degree examination and joined me in Delhi and we resumed our family life sadly interrupted by the Aligarh events two years earlier. I was blessed with a son, Ramesh, four years after marriage. Life at home and work in the law faculty appeared to be progressing well after some turbulence. I wanted to be a great teacher and sought advice from elders including the then Dean, Dr. P.K. Tripathi. I had a good friend Mr. Narasimha Swamy Mysore who, fresh from Harvard, joined the Delhi Law School as a Lecturer like me. He was living with me in the Jubilee Hall quarters for sometime. We jointly taught a course which was newly introduced for which there were no takers among the senior faculty. It was on "Law relating to Government Control of Business". We assiduously collected all cases on the subject, edited them and distributed to students with a view to teach the course through the "Socratic Method". In a series of faculty seminars during those days, Visiting Professors from America had introduced us to the Socratic Method of law teaching. Moreover, Narasimha Swamy had studied under that method for his LL.M. in U.S.A. Together we did what we thought was a great job and earned some reputation for excellence in teaching. The Dean appreciated it. Eastern Law Book Co. came forward to publish the study materials we put together in the form of a book titled "Law Relating to Government Control of Business" which sold very well and ran into several editions. I became an author and got noted in legal circles even outside Delhi.

Simultaneously both of us were involved with teaching of another new course called "Law and Poverty", a subject which assumed quick popularity with students. The materials we put together for teaching, that course was picked up by another leading publisher from Bombay, N.M. Tripathi & Co. who brought out my second book on "Law and Poverty" of which I was a co-author.

Delhi University Law Faculty is one of the biggest law faculties in India. It had strength of 70-80 law teachers at any given time. It is one of the most vibrating departments and always on the vanguard of any movements in the University. I had the privilege of the association of some of the best legal minds in the country. These include Prof. P.K. Tripathi, Prof. Lotika Sarkar, Prof. Jaffer Hussain, Prof. Errabi, Prof. B.B. Pande, Prof. D.K. Singh, Prof. Upendra Baxi, Prof. Mool Chand Sharma, Prof. V.K. Dikshit to name a few teachers. I have a special admiration for Prof. Baxi for his scholarship in the field of law and his capacity to inspire students to look at law beyond the conventional boundaries of Statutes and precedents. The model law curriculum prepared under his Chairmanship by the UGC has influenced legal learning in significant ways. He deserved to be appointed to the Supreme Court from among the category of jurists.

American Visits and Connections

The 1960s have been a period of reforms in legal education in Delhi University. The Gajendragadkar report on legal education at Delhi had inspired authorities to look for new initiatives in the University. The Ford Foundation support to introduce changes in curriculum, pedagogy and faculty development brought about a series of interaction between teachers of Delhi Law Faculty and some of the senior professors of Harvard, Columbia, Michigan and Yale Law Schools. Professor Arthur Murphy from Columbia University Law School at New York and Professor Kenneth Penegar from the Southern Methodist University Law School have been my colleagues for a couple of years between 1968-'70 who have been co-teaching with me a newly introduced course on "Law and Poverty" and two conventional courses on Criminal Law and Procedure. Through a series of Faculty Seminars and Workshops, the American colleagues demonstrated the content and delivery of case method of law teaching and strategies for introducing it progressively in Delhi University. With Prof. Penegar, I developed study materials of selected cases in Criminal Law. We edited them and prepared key questions to be asked in the class to guide the discussion to desired ends while letting students to learn the law from actual cases and judgements. Materials were cyclostyled and distributed to students in advance asking them to come prepared with study of facts, issues and decisions on them. The classes turned out to be interesting and lively and the time available (50 minutes) was found insufficient as so many students, otherwise passive listeners, got involved in heated arguments both on facts and reasoning. This was indeed a turning point in law teaching at Delhi University. My own interest to learn more about what the Americans call the "Socratic method" grew stronger particularly after looking at some of the standard "Cases and Materials" developed by American law teachers on different subjects in substantive and procedural laws.

In the summer of 1969 I received an invitation to join a Workshop on Law and Social Science Research at the North-Western University Law School at Chicago to be conducted by two American sociologists-turned law teachers Prof. Richard Schwartz and Prof. Marc Galanter. Dr. L.M. Singhvi, the renowned jurist and parliamentarian, whom I met in few seminars and conferences in Delhi earlier, was responsible for sponsoring me to this workshop. There were two other participants also from India, one who is now a judge of the Indian Supreme Court (Hon'ble Mr. Justice Dalveer Bhandari) and the other a Sociologist who was then the Director of the Institute of Parliamentary Studies in Delhi (Dr. G.R.S. Rao). This was my first visit to the United States and was overjoyed at the prospects of visiting the "land of opportunities" though only for few days. The menu that Schwartz and Galanter provided at the workshop was a rich and varied one, full of intellectual challenges that law teachers trained in the conventional mould seldom come across. We were invited to look at law from the perspective of social and behavioural scientists and critique its goals and methods. My education in political science did help me to catch up with the instruction and develop my own intellectual kit as a teacher and researcher.

Soon afterwards, under the Faculty exchange programme Delhi University had under Ford Foundation support, I was selected to spend an year in Columbia University Law School at New York, where Prof. Arthur Murphy my colleague at Delhi for two years was teaching. I was not expected to work for any degree but only to observe, critique and audit the American system of legal education. Besides, I was to give few Seminars on selected topics to the Faculty and students and to write a report on my impressions. Living in the International Students' House a couple of blocks away from the law school in up town New York, I enjoyed my stay though the freedom of movement was rather restricted because of security concerns and paucity of funds. Nevertheless, towards the end of my stay, I took a month-long travel as you please 100 dollar Greyhound ticket and visited more than thirty states across America and Canada, visiting cities and towns during the day and travelling by bus during nights. The American Council of International Education provided logistic support, arranged stay with American families in few places, civic reception in one or two cities (!). It was great education of the country and its people which opportunity seldom one gets unless one is able to devote considerable time and money.

Under the Fulbright Programme with a Fellowship from American Council of Learned Societies I had again occasion to spend another year in the United States in late 1970s. I spent part of the time in the west coast (Columbia and New York Universities) and the rest of the time in the east coast (University of California at Los Angeles). The time was devoted more to learn about the clinical methodology used in teaching skills to the law student and in exploring the interface between law and social sciences research. On a few more occasions I made short visits to the United States, once to present a paper on Legal Aid in a South Asian Law Conference at Berkeley and a second time to participate in a Law and Development Conference at Wiscosin.

My final encounter with American legal education has been a teaching assignment in the Washington University Law School at St. Louis where I taught a two credit course on "Equality and Affirmative Action : Indian and U.S. Experience" jointly with my friend and colleague Prof. Clark Cunningham. It was a rewarding experience interacting with students from a dozen countries and examining the limits and limitations of law in bringing about equality in unequal societies. I was elated to find that the students at the end of the course ranked my performance with the highest grade. I was doubly happy to find that an article which myself and Cunningham jointly wrote during the period was published as a lead article in the Michigan Law Journal.

A Turning Point in Teaching of Criminal Law

A touching incident happened in the Delhi Law Faculty during those days which opened my eyes and questioned my method of teaching Criminal Law and Criminal Procedure, the subjects of my specialization. The year was 1967 and the month was November when Delhi usually changed to the winter season. One morning in November, a middle aged lady with three children walked into the Law faculty seeking assistance to trace her husband, a railway employee in Hyderabad, who went missing in Delhi six weeks ago while seeking to get some service benefits from his employer, the Ministry of Railways. In a letter to her from Delhi, he conveyed his frustration in not being able to meet the Minister of Railways and his pathetic condition in

Delhi streets. The Dean Prof. P.K. Tripathi to whom she approached with a letter from a M.P. (Member of Parliament) from A.P. (Andhra Pradesh) asked me and Narasimha Swamy to see what could be done to help the woman. A live case, a client in distress and legal aid from academic lawyers who had neither practiced law nor understood the way the game was played in real life. We took it as a challenge, consulted some colleagues and students and decided to take up the matter in the cause of justice to the poor. We had no means to identify him except through her, as there was not even a photograph of the man. The initial plan was to inform the police and to go with her to Tihar Jail, one of the places where persons found missing in the capital might land up for all sorts of reasons. Our first task was to ensure the safety of the woman and her children. They could speak neither Hindi nor had any place to stay in Delhi. She managed the previous night at railway waiting hall. We decided to ask the Member of Parliament from Andhra Pradesh who referred her to law faculty to accommodate them for a few days. We left the children at MPs residence in South Avenue and left for Tihar Jail for physical verification. We were turned away from Tihar on the ground that we did not have proper authorization. We then got permission the next day and took the rounds of several cells with jail officials. As there were no details of arrest with us, the jail records could not help. Finally the woman detected her husband in a half-naked condition who had shown no emotions on his face. We were doubtful about his identity as he was not talking to his wife whom he saw suddenly after nearly six weeks of separation that too in an unexpected environment of a jail! It took time for him to digest the presence of his wife and there was an emotional reunion of the family. On checking jail records we found that he was sent there by the Parliament Street Police Station under some preventive sections of the Criminal Procedure Code (moving around in suspicious circumstances in Connaught Place jewelry shop). On verifying with Court record we discovered that he was being routinely remanded for recording evidence of the Investigating Officer (IO). We pleaded with the Magistrate for his discharge. He ordered another date for the I.O. to appear failing which he promised to consider our plea for discharge. As before, the police was not interested in an apparently false case and the under-trial was unconditionally discharged on the 8th day of our involvement. To our utter surprise the man was refusing to leave Court unless the 600 rupees that police allegedly took from his possession on the day of arrest was returned to him. There was no record to that effect. He said he was in a depressed mood and was sitting in a posh restaurant in Connaught Place taking coffee for long hours. He picked a quarrel with the manager who called the police to remove him. The police arrested and took him to the station where they removed the money from his possession and framed a charge under Section 109, Cr. P.C. apparently to cover up their misdeeds. We could not verify the facts; but there was no reason to disbelieve him as he was a permanent railway employee at Hyderabad and came to Delhi for genuine reasons of getting some service benefits by meeting the Railway Minister. The Magistrate asked us to mobilize some money and send the man with his family back to his home State which we did.

We reflected on the prevailing system of Criminal justice which could detain people endlessly on flimsy grounds, gave impunity to erring officials and offered no compensation even for illegal acts. We had a seminar in the Faculty on our experience with the case and we decided to start a legal aid clinic to help the poor in need of our services. The first Legal Aid Clinic was started in the Delhi University in 1968. I realized the futility of teaching law from the books only without exposing students to the facts and procedure on the ground. We declared that when we teach procedural laws, we will take the students to courts where law in action takes place. The exposure to the courts demonstrated to them how things are worked out whether in case of arrest or bail, conviction or acquittal. Thereafter revisiting the legal provisions would make them understand the processes of administration of justice. The idea was executed involving students in the paralegal services particularly to the poor with a view to enable them to understand the social context of the legal processes and to expose them to the 'poverty' of law itself. It was a turning point in my life as a teacher. The laws like criminal law, family law, labour law etc., are centered around human relationships and emotions. Any misapplication will shatter the lives and ruin the families. By teaching of law from the text books or decided cases only, the social context will be missing in the process of education. There is need to observe the role of law as regulator of human relations. I published an article on my experience in the hope that others similarly placed would be persuaded to look at what they were teaching from a realistic functional perspective.

The 1970s saw me maturing as a teacher and an activist for reforms in legal education, legal aid and legal profession. The system of legal education that I saw in the United States and the few experiments at innovations in teaching I had at Delhi, made me impatient to seek more changes though, as a junior teacher in a large faculty, I was not in a position to accomplish anything like that. As the saying goes, pessimists would find difficulties in opportunity and optimists would find opportunities even in difficulty. I belonged to the latter category, or so I believed. The All India Law Teachers Association held its annual conference in Delhi in 1972 of which I was an active organizer. I pushed an agenda of reforms in legal education which attracted attention of even the peers and critics. At the end of the jamboree I was elected the Secretary General of the Association, a position which enabled my voice to be heard throughout the law teaching community.

In the same year under Mrs. Indira Gandhi's Twenty-Point Programme on "Garibi Hatao", an expert committee was constituted to examine the idea of justice to the poor. Justice V.R. Krishna Iyer who was then member of the Law Commission of India was its Chairman and to my pleasant surprise I found myself appointed a member of the high-powered Legal Aid Committee. Though I have heard of Justice Iyer as a former Minister of Kerala under the first Communist government, I had no opportunity to meet him before; and suddenly I became an "expert" in his Committee ! I assumed that the noises I made through newspapers on my experiments in teaching a new course on Law & Poverty and in organizing a Student Legal Services Clinic at Delhi Law Faculty projected me as an academic with ideas on justice to the poor. In fact, the then Union Law Minister Mr. H.R. Gokale wrote the Foreword to my book on "Legal Aid and Legal Education" which was a collection of articles on involvement of law students in legal aid support services and clinical legal education. In short, outside law teaching, legal aid became my favourite activity which later on made me to play a significant role in the Committee for Implementing Legal Aid Schemes (CILAS) set up by the Government of India under the Chairmanship of Justice P.N. Bhagwati, Judge of the Supreme court of India.

From accumulated knowledge and experience in this direction in various countries of the world particularly the United States and Canada, one can reasonably suggest that the institution of legal aid clinics is an ideal and necessary device to impart education while serving the society and achieving in the process revolutionary reforms both in legal education and in administration of justice. More than anything else American's progress and prosperity can be attributed to its system of higher education and India has many lessons to learn from it. The few changes that have come about in Indian legal education can largely be attributed to the role played by dozens of American educated Indian law teachers including Professors R.U. Singh, G.S. Sharma, Anandjee, P.K. Tripathi, Hafeezul Rehman, K.S. Murty and others. I have myself borrowed and developed the clinical method of law teaching from my repeated exposure to experiments in several law schools in America and interaction with distinguished clinicians like Prof. Clark Cunningham from Georgia Law School and Prof. Frank Bloch from the Vanderbilt Law School. Furthermore, one can say that the affinity between the two countries, India and USA, is founded more on commitment to constitutionalism, democracy and rule of law rather than on any other factor in history or politics. With globalization of legal services, this relationship is bound to grow stronger to the advantage of rule of law and democracy everywhere.

Opportunity to Implement Ideas on Reforming Legal Education

As luck would have it, in 1973 the Pondicherry Government was proposing to establish a Law College in the Union Territory and they sought my services as its Principal on deputation from Delhi University. By that time I had my first promotion in Delhi University and was posted as a Reader (Associate Professor) and the Principalship of a College was in a sense a quick second promotion for me. I consulted my wife who was keen to go as the place was hallowed by the names of Sri Aurobindo and the Mother and was nearer to our hometown in Kerala. I went to Pondicherry in early 1974 and was received by my namesake Mr. A.C. Menon, the then Law Secretary to the Government. The leisurely pace of life of the people in the area, the remnants of French culture in the town and the serenity surrounding the Ashram and the Lord Ganesha temple impressed us greatly.

It was Sri Aurobindo, the great patriot, philosopher and saint who said that man is capable of evolving into superman because of the innate abilities already in him, waiting to be developed through pursuit of knowledge and perfection. This is what modern science is also demonstrating in contemporary times. Education, after all as Swami Vivekananda said long ago, is the process of bringing out the infinite potential that is latent in every human being. My son started attending the 'Cluny' school in Pondy and I got extremely busy in developing a vision for the college and an academic agenda to begin with.

The law college was affiliated to Madras University and therefore had to necessarily follow that curriculum and academic schedule. What was left to me was the infra-structure development, faculty and student selection, co-curricular activities and most importantly, method of teaching. Imbued with the idea of "Socratic method" tried out in Delhi University and the experiment in involving the law students in legal aid clinics, I made it a point to institutionalize these pedagogic innovations in the Pondicherry law college programmes right from the beginning. I carefully selected a team of teachers, interviewed each and every student admitted, organized an intensive orientation course for the newly admitted students and started my first attempt as an administrator and institution-builder in the former French colony. I made it a point to cultivate the French identity of the place in the College by starting a Diploma in French Law which I ran with the help of the then District and Session Judge of Pondicherry Dr. David Annoussamy who was to a large extent, instrumental in getting the law college established in the city.

Pondicherry was a great experience and four years went off quickly at the end of which Delhi University called me back by refusing to extend the deputation. By that time the Pondicherry Law College earned a reputation for quality legal education in Southern India and attracted some highly talented students from all States in the region. One of the finest law library got set up in Pondicherry which was the envy of law colleges in that part of the country.

On the request of Annamalai University in Tamilnadu I agreed to be the first Dean of the newly opened Law Faculty at Chidambaram, yet another recognition of the academic work getting appreciated by quarters beyond one's immediate work place. I was also appointed in a Committee by Dr. Malcom Adiseshiah, the then Vice Chancellor of Madras University, to re-structure legal education under Advocate General Govind Swaminathan as its Chairman. I became more and more visible as a legal academic particularly in South India for my iconoclastic instincts in breaking new ground on the structure and method of legal education. Surely and steadily, it became a mission with me.

On the home front, I was blessed with a daughter, our second child who unfortunately developed the dreaded disease of 'meningitis'. She survived after a long period of care and treatment. My wife took the whole burden of looking after the two children and managing the home for which I had no time nor expertise. I often used to travel to many places on academic work leaving the family alone. Mr. A.C. Menon and family who was then Secretary to Pondy Government helped us in all our difficulties in an otherwise unfamiliar environment. The revered Mother of Aurobindo Ashram died during that period. Nevertheless Pondicherry continued as a tourist destination and a window of French Culture in India.

Back to Delhi and Stint with the Bar Council of India Trust

In 1978 I joined back the Campus Law Centre of the Delhi Law Faculty and soon got involved in legal education reform and development of law school involvement in legal aid services. In 1979 I was tempted by an offer from the Bar Council of India to assist the

Council in its tasks of maintaining legal education standards, imparting continuing education to the bar, editing and publishing a Bar Council journal and advising it on professional development activities. The Chairman was Mr. Ram Jethmalani who persuaded me to join the organization as the first Secretary of the Bar Council of India Trust which was dormant after its establishment a couple of years earlier. The office was in a building across the Supreme Court and I had to travel a long way from Ashok Vihar where I had bought a DDA flat on long term instalment payment basis. My colleagues in the law faculty thought the Bar Council job was a Secretarial job which they felt demeaning for an academic person to hold. In my enthusiasm to co-opt the Bar Council, the statutory body in charge of legal education, to my ideas of legal education reform I thought it was a God-sent opportunity and I took the plunge taking leave without pay from Delhi University. My wife supported me in my decision though in the process her burden to manage the home front increased substantially.

In 1979 I was also selected for the Senior Fulbright Programme under which I was given a Fellowship as a Visiting Scholar by the American Council of Learned Societies. I spent an year at Columbia Law School, New York and visited several campuses to learn different techniques of legal education and professional development.

A great tragedy in my life struck me on the eve of my departure to America. My revered mother from whom I took blessings for the U.S. trip a fortnight earlier, suddenly passed away. I cancelled my ticket to New York and rushed to Trivandrum. As fate would have it, there was no direct flight to Trivandrum from Delhi and when I landed in Madras, the only onward flight to Trivandrum had already departed. I heard an announcement over the public address system at the airport that the flight to Coimbatore was ready for departure which I took and landed there. The only escape from there was by train which took almost ten hours to take me to Trivandrum. I informed my sisters of my having left Delhi by flight and they were waiting for my arrival for the cremation without knowing my travails in missing the connecting flights. When I informed them that I was in a train from Coimbatore they were surprised and worried. Nevertheless they waited keeping the body surrounded by ice slabs and chanting prayers continuously. It was a harrowing journey I could never forget. The only satisfaction was that I could perform the last rites which a son owed to his mother. Though I lost the physical presence of my mother, she continued to guide me in all my endeavours with that unlimited love and forgiveness which a Mother alone could give.

Legal education has been in total disarray since Independence and neither the organized profession nor the University system could do anything worthwhile to arrest the decline in standards. There was not even one institution among the couple of hundred law colleges in the country which could claim some degree of professionalism and scholarship. Thousands of ill-equipped, unemployable law degree holders were being turned out every year to become, as the Law Commission observed, "half-baked lawyers who act as touts and parasites in society". The malaise had its adverse impact on administration of justice and in governance itself. Still, Universities were reluctant to change either because of fear of student unrest or inability to organize the resources needed for reform. It was in this context that the Bar Council of India decided to start a model Law University to show the law teaching institutions how legal education had to be organized to make it socially relevant and professionally useful. It fell to my lot to conceive the new University, assemble the resources necessary and accomplish the goal of putting in place a working model of a centre of excellence in legal education.

Discussing the character of law colleges at the time of Independence, the Law Commission of India in its Fourteenth Report (Setalvad Commission 1958) stated that "the main purpose of university legal education seems hitherto to have been not the teaching of law as a science or as a branch of learning, but merely imparting to students a knowledge of certain principles and provisions of law to enable them to enter the legal profession .. .. .. Part-time institutions have been regarded as sufficient for this purpose. Those institutions seemed to have suited both the teacher and the taught. Most of the students who attended the morning and evening classes conducted by those institutions were in employment somewhere or prosecuted some other post-graduate study while the teachers in law were generally practicing lawyers who had to attend to their professional business during office hours."

While the Bar Council of India succeeded in bringing about some discipline on the academic spheres, it failed miserably on the organizational and professional aspects. Thus a three-year programme of legal education after graduation was accepted throughout the country by 1967 and a uniform curriculum comprising fourteen compulsory subjects and a minimum of two optional subjects came to be adopted by all the universities imparting legal education. These are indeed substantial achievements in the academic content of legal education particularly in comparison to the deplorable condition which existed before. But very soon some greedy college managements and a class of professionally unsuccessful advocates organized themselves to defeat every one of these achievements by disregarding the wholesome provisions of the Bar Council Rules on Legal Education. The control mechanism through inspection of law colleges provided for in the Rules did not succeed in arresting mushroom growth of teaching shops claiming to be professional centres of legal education.

Some university departments of law like those of Delhi and Chandigarh, Banaras and Aligarh are, or can be, excellent centers of legal education comparable to some of the best in other countries. Similarly, some Government and private law colleges are also capable of becoming first-rate institutions for professional education but failed in that regard due to a variety of external factors.

Given motivated students and qualified teachers, legal education can improve considerably. There are a variety of supporting factors which facilitate the process which are of great importance and which have been neglected for too long. In this connection the problem of lack of physical and intellectual facilities and educational environment warranted priority attention. As observed by the Law Commission (14th Report), most law colleges do not have either buildings or libraries. Classes are held, if at all, in mornings or evenings in premises wholly inadequate for meaningful education. Colleges have neither student hostels nor playgrounds. Libraries are non-existent and wherever they exist, they lack standard law books and law reports.

On my return to India from America I took up the Bar Council assignment and served there for nearly three years. That was the period when the Five Year Integrated LL.B. programme was conceived by the Bar Council in consultation with Universities to replace the 3 year post-graduate LL.B. Course. I did a survey of the status of legal education in every state which gave a vivid picture of the chaos that prevailed. The findings of the survey were published as a book by the Bar Council of India in 1982. I travelled widely in different states on behalf of the Bar Council Trust conducting continuing education courses for lawyers and seminars on the integrated five-year course for law teachers. In the process, I canvassed wide support for the 5-year integrated LL.B. course. There was resistance to the proposal from vested interests in some places. The Bar Council of India, despite opposition from within its own ranks, proposed 1982 as the cut off year for switching over to the 5 year LL.B. course. A petition was filed in Court challenging the authority of the Bar Council to prescribe a 5 year course when the Advocates Act allowed only a 3 year course. To overcome the legal lacuna the Council argued that the first two years of the 5 year course were meant to teach non-law courses which the student anyway was required to study in his graduation as a pre-law requirement. Udaipur University in Rajasthan was the first to introduce the new Scheme in 1983. Though many others followed, the majority including my own University (Delhi) refused to switch over and prevailed on the Bar Council to let both the streams (3 year course as well as 5 year course) continue, a disaster which could not be avoided.

Meanwhile a section of the Bar Councillors led by M/s Ram Jethmalani, Ranjit Mohanty and V.R. Reddy mooted the idea of sponsoring a model law school by the Bar Council of India for which a society was registered including me also as a member. A blue print for a National Law School was prepared with assistance from several law teachers including Professor Upendra Baxi, my colleague in the Law Faculty of Delhi University. The U.G.C. was not willing to give it a Deemed University status under the UGC Act despite a favourable opinion given by the then Attorney General of India. As an alternative, Bar Council had sounded their State Units to find out whether any of the State Governments would give it an independent statutory status and would give land and infra-structure resources. Karnataka Bar Council was successful in persuading their Government not only to give a legislation giving University status but also temporary accommodation and land for building the campus. The National Law School of India University was formally announced to be located at Bangalore and efforts to find the Director who would establish it and develop it as the "Harvard of the East" had begun.

Experience as Head of Campus Law Centre, Delhi University

Meanwhile at the end of my three-year tenure with the Bar Council of India, I re-joined Delhi University as Head of the Campus Law Centre, a position assigned on rotation to one of the senior teachers in the Centre. Two incidents which happened in my professional career really pained me at that time though both incidents finally strengthened my resolve to stand by principles and not yield to pressures, threats and unfair treatments. The first related to my appointment as a full professor. When vacancies were advertised for Professorship which was the most coveted position in an academic's career, I had also applied as I fulfilled the eligibility conditions. The University, probably on the advice of the Dean, took the view that I did not fulfill all the eligibility requirements as they found my three-year tenure at the Bar Council of India as neither teaching nor research experience. My representation to the contrary did not convince them and they refused to call me for the interview. I challenged the University's decision through a writ petition in the Delhi High Court to the surprise of my colleagues and the Delhi

University authorities. My lawyer was my former student at Pondicherry Law College Mr. R. Venkatramani who had just shifted his practice to Delhi from Madras. Together we prepared the documentation. Court admitted the matter and issued notice. Tense moments for me and my wife who accompanied me to the hearings, seeing a Court proceedings for the first time in her life. The Delhi High Court decided the matter against the University. I was called for the interview, got selected and appointed Professor in Delhi University, a position for which I got selected in Aligarh Muslim University, thirteen years earlier in 1968 ! That is life all about; do not let injustice lying down and if truth is on your side nothing can stop you from getting what you deserve. God is indeed on the side of Truth and Justice.

As Professor-in-Charge of Campus Law Centre I wanted, to change the ways in which teaching, administration, co-curricular activities, discipline etc. were organized. I got the campus cleaned up of its wild growth, got the building white-washed and painted to give a new look. The money that was available was very limited and they had to be utilized for academic activities rather than beautification, my colleagues cautioned. I started with regular faculty meetings in which I raised every issue of teaching or administration for open discussion and collective decision. It did receive appreciation and support. We resolved to stick to agreed academic schedule and insist on some degree of personal discipline including punctuality from teachers, students and staff. Some did not like it; but they could not do anything about it. In this regard my colleagues particularly Jaffer Hussain, Errabbi, Ahmed Siddique, Solil Paul, Ishar, Sethi and Gupta were of great help. We decided to print the cases in each subject for distribution to students ending the system of cyclostyling, a clumsy and costly process, seldom clear and readable and never made available in time. It was a great step forward in instructional reform. Strikes and boycotts which were the order of the day were controlled with introduction of many co-curricular programmes, particularly moot courts, mock trials, debates and legal aid clinic activities. As I got a University accommodation by then just across the road in Maurice Nagar, I could be present all the time in the campus, and could be personally involved in the activities. Things started looking up in the first year of my tenure as Professor-in-Charge. Towards the end of the second year, a conflict with a section of students shook me up very badly which still linger in my thoughts even after 25 years.

The year was 1985. The practice of agitations to prolong admission process and postpone examination schedules was the order of the day. As usual a section of students led by a couple of so-called leaders (not the duly elected Union) approached me asking for postponement of examination by two weeks. I tried to reason with them which they refused to listen. They gave me time to reconsider the matter and came back to get my response the next day. I was not prepared to dilute the disciplinary environment being built up after great deal of collective efforts including a vast section of the student body. I ascertained that the majority of students were not keen on postponement. I therefore refused their demand rather firmly which they could not stomach. They were determined to get it postponed and they approached a section of teachers. I was informed that some teachers were sympathetic to their cause and some even advised them to continue their agitation. Be that as it may, tension was building up with students and teachers divided on the issue. I raised the matter in a specially convened faculty meeting. The opinion was unanimous that there was no valid reason to postpone and the exam should be held on schedule and the administration should be prepared for all eventualities.

The turn of events angered the leadership of unruly students who found their credibility being at stake and decided to resort to violent methods. They got the gate locked and prevented entry of students, staff and teachers. I got it opened and requested students to attend classes. I told them that exam would be held on schedule and any attempt to disturb it would be put down firmly. I got the posters and placards of the agitators removed which angered them more. They barged into my office, asked the visitors sitting with me to go out of the room and bolted door from inside. Outside, my office staff was stunned and watched the developments with fear. They reported it to the teachers who were taking classes in the first and second floors of the building. Many of them came down to see and possibly prevent any untoward incidents but could not get into my office where the drama was unfolding. The leader of the group sat on my table pushing aside the papers on it. He asked me in an authoritative tone to sign the paper he brought announcing postponement of exam. Trembling with fear I became totally benumbed not knowing what to do. After a few minutes of silence during which the group was throwing abuses in Punjabi at me, I mumbled a few words to convey that I would not do it as the Faculty took a considered decision against it in the interests of students themselves. From the way I expressed they could understand that I was under severe stress and fearful of the consequences. They said that they were on a 'Dharna' in my office and would not let me go out of it unless I agreed to their demand. The ordeal continued for over two hours with students collecting outside shouting slogans in a threatening posture. Apparently someone informed the police who had come outside the

Law Faculty building expecting to receive a written complaint and permission to deal with it as a law and order issue.

Inside my office, the impatient and frustrated leaders changed tactics. The leader of the group collected an empty cola bottle broke it by striking against my table and pointed towards me. I thought I would be seriously injured in the next few moments. No, it was not to be. He shouted at me saying that he would injure himself with the broken bottle and would file an FIR to the effect that I caused the grievous injury on him citing his companions as eye-witnesses. What an intelligent application of law which I taught him? Well, hearing the shouts and breaking of glass, the teachers asked the police to break in and save their colleague taken hostage inside. The police got in; the students moved out and merged with the crowd outside. Police gathered the details and asked me permission to proceed and asked for a written complaint from me. Suddenly it dawned on me that if I started the criminal proceedings, the academic atmosphere could be vitiated and I too would not have the peace of mind. The episode I experienced at Aligarh during student riots came to my mind. I told the police that it was an internal matter which could be settled between the administration and students. In fact, the students involved in the episode expected me to act differently and were pleasantly surprised when the police were asked to go without even a complaint being filed with them. Some of them immediately rushed back to my office and apologized on behalf of the rowdy elements amongst them. The examination was held on schedule in which even the agitators also participated perhaps with a feeling of guilt. I told the story to my wife who could not believe that all that happened was true. She prevailed on me to relinquish charge as the Head of the Department which I did and thus ended my tenure on educational administration in Delhi University.

After several years of the incident I met one of those students in Delhi who introduced himself as a member of the Bar Council of Delhi. On enquiry I found out that he was also a member of the Disciplinary Committee of the Bar Council. I laughed myself and wished him well in guarding the ethics of the profession!

Chapter III

Leading the National Law School Movement

LEADING THE NATIONAL LAW SCHOOL MOVEMENT

1980s have been an exciting period in the history of legal education in India. The Bar Council of India made a bold attempt to change the structure and content of law studies by introducing the Five-Year Integrated LL.B. programme which brought in social sciences, English language and skills training as integral to the learning of law. The Bar Council distinguished professional legal education from liberal (academic) learning of law and left the latter entirely to the discretion of Universities and Colleges. A system of inspection and certification of law colleges was put in place under which the Council weeded out some teaching shops which were exploiting students and diluting standards. The Curriculum Development Committee set up by the University Grants Commission came up with a new set of courses providing an integrated approach to post-graduate legal studies. Universities like Delhi introduced under support from Ford Foundation, programmes of exchange of teachers with leading American law schools and adopted "Case Method" of teaching in certain subjects. And above all, the agenda of a model law school long cherished by the Bar Council to act as a pace-setter in legal education reforms got established during the period.

Invitation to set up the "Harvard of the East"

The Bar Council of India approached me in 1985 to find out whether I would be prepared to take the responsibility to conceive, establish and develop the National Law School as an independent university heralding a decisive change in professional legal education in the country. After some hesitation I took up the challenge in early 1986 to see whether some degree of quality and excellence could be brought into legal education as it was happening in medicine, engineering and management. The then Chairman of the Bar Council who issued the order of appointment to me as the first Director of the proposed National Law School was Mr. V.C. Mishra, a wily lawyer from

Allahabad who later got into trouble with the Supreme Court for quarrelling with judges of the U.P. High Court.

There is a continuing controversy among legal educators in India regarding the goal of legal education—one section holding it to be strictly concerned with producing legal practitioners (perhaps the conventional lawyer who is an expert in litigation—oriented skills), while another section advocating a wider role in which the lawyer is equipped with divergent skills, perspectives and tools of analysis with a view to make him a policy maker, administrator and social engineer. The latter group contends that with the fast-changing socio-economic structure and methods of social ordering and conflict management, the traditional role of the lawyer is of diminishing value or at least that the new role of lawyer in society calls for skills, knowledge and techniques far more diverse and comprehensive than his traditional counterpart. Depending upon the emphasis one gives to one or the other of the two approaches, one's concept of legal education including curriculum, teaching methods and examination system varied.

The initial problem of getting independent identity as a full-fledged university was solved when the Karnataka Government promulgated an ordinance named National Law School of India University Act (NLSIU). I was named its first Director. Taking five years' extra-ordinary leave from Delhi University, I moved to Bangalore leaving my family back in Delhi. Living in a room in the old MLA's hostel I started exploring a temporary location for the University and ways to mobilize funds for setting up the essential infra-structure. Mr. R.V. Krishnappa who retired from the Agricultural University at Bangalore was appointed as Registrar. A few rooms got allotted at a corner of the Central College Campus. They were made up to serve as the office of NLSIU. An amount of Rs. 25 lakhs sanctioned by the Karnataka Government and an equal sum promised by the Bar Council of India Trust was to constitute the initial fund of the University. I was asked by the sponsors and promoters of the enterprise to mobilize resources and build infra-structure pending which to manage running expenditure with the available funds of Rs. 50 lakhs. A tall order in organizing a centre for excellence in professional legal education!

Elders in the teaching profession did advise me against taking such a huge risk of floating a law school without funds or infra-structure. At the same time I was personally excited of having got an opportunity to build something new which had been the dream of lawyers and educationists for quite sometime. Some inner voice kept telling me that I would succeed and I should be prepared for sacrifices and many risks in the process. With the encouragement of my wife, the advice of people like Mr. Justice V.R. Krishna Iyer and Ram Jethmalani and the blessings of my mother, I initiated a series of steps to put things together and to start the classes in the summer of 1987, within one year of my assuming charge as the Director.

Teaching is a noble activity. It involves a great deal of sacrifices and total commitment to the welfare of the students. It cannot offer big money as in some other professions. These days it does not even command respect from the students. Its greatest reward is the promotion of socially relevant scholarship and intellectual enlightenment in partnership with the students. To be able to perform in contemporary times, the teacher has to have strong commitment to the pursuit of scholarship and the sense of humility to learn even from his students. Knowledge is such a thing that the more you have it, the more you realize how little you know. That makes you humble and puts you in the position of a learner even while you teach.

All caution was taken in selecting the faculty members. A faculty of twelve persons was carefully selected after a global search and they were persuaded to share the dream and be prepared for the initial sacrifices involved in a new venture. This was organized through a six month-long programme of meetings, workshops, intensive study sessions and interactive seminars with a cross-section of lawyers, law teachers and educational administrators. The idea was to motivate and commit the team for a great leap forward and to get them abandon personal agendas at least till the time the primary mission was accomplished. Yes, even the basic comforts of housing and transportation could not be provided and the salary offered was consolidated amounts much less than what they could have had in their parent institutions. Looking back at the period between 1986 and 1991 I am amazed on how teachers and staff worked with such dedication and sacrifice for the common cause of building an institution for which there was neither a model nor a clear design. It was indeed a dream full of ideals in which the dreamers were not prepared to accept excuses, alibis or explanations for missing the target. There was no vacation or long holidays and the academic year extended throughout the calendar year. Fellow travelers in Bangalore University had no clue of what was happening and were surprised at the way a handful of men and women were going about setting up what they called "a University within a University"! (NLSIU was then located in a corner of Central College which was part of Bangalore University).

Faculty is central to run an educational institution. Faculty meetings were held on regular basis. Every issue was tabled and discussed, there were arguments at times and ultimately it was the collective decision process that helped to build the institution. In the first year there were more teachers and fewer subjects to teach. The idea of co-operative teaching was introduced. Even the law teachers taught the non-law subjects like History, political science etc. A totally different work culture was developed in the academic and non-academic aspects. For the first time trimester system was introduced in legal education. The academic calendar was prepared in the beginning itself and there was strict adherence to the schedule and total transparency was maintained in all activities.

It is too long a story to be narrated here in all its details. I would like to highlight some academic and few administrative innovations introduced in the making of National Law School which gave it a unique character and impressed the world outside. First, the work culture which made a difference in higher education. NLSIU had over 300 working days in a year organized in three academic terms. Being a residential university such a rigorous Calendar gave value addition to learning in a number of ways. Second, the curriculum provided for specialization in a number of emerging areas of law with inter-disciplinary focus. This was possible because of the three terms for study every year and a rich optional curriculum seldom provided in a law school before. Third, the teaching methods combined a variety of learning techniques with heavy emphasis on research-based, experiential learning, employing individual projects, externship and clinical programmes. Fourth, the examination system was a continuing process throughout the term enabling the students to know and correct the progress in learning. It was a transparent process combining theory with practice conducted by the teacher herself in each subject. Finally, a host of co-curricular activities, some of them with academic credit, provided opportunities for self-expression and for all round development of the students in the course of five years they were in residence with the University. The selection process was entirely based on an admission test with reservations for S.Cs and S.Ts. The weaker students received individual assistance through tutorials, mentorship and remedial courses. The result was almost one hundred per cent success with hardly anyone failing or dropping out from the course!

Though it was a daunting task to start a University in a dilapidated building, we were not in despair. In the first year, only 40 students were admitted for B.A., LL.B. (Hons.) Course. There was no library. However, the first batch when they participated in the Phillip Jesssop International Moot Court Competition they marked their presence without any supporting facility. Really it was hard times for the first batch of the students. It was in 1992 the 'University' was shifted to the new campus while the construction work was still going on. In fact, there was reluctance from the students to move to the new campus because it was too far away from the city. A decisive stand made all to shift to the new campus.

On the administrative side, NLSIU took care to ensure that the total administrative and supporting staff did not exceed the total number of teachers in the University. When I left the University in 1997, NLSIU had nearly 40 teachers (including the visiting faculty) and about 32 administrative staff including the Registrar, catering to a little over 500 students (not including another 500 students in the Distance Learning Programmes). It shows the total dedication of the administrative staff who would work overtime without any rewards when circumstances demanded it. There was no occasion during my twelve year tenure as the head of NLSIU when I had to close down the institution or take disciplinary action against any of the administrative staff. It speaks volumes on the discipline and work culture of the staff, students and teachers and reveals the secret of the success story that was NLSIU.

On the financial front, the story had its ups and downs. There were a couple of occasions when we felt that the University might have to be closed down and the students transferred to other law colleges of their choice. The source of income was the one time grant of Rs. 50 lakhs from the BCI Trust and the Karnataka Government and the tuition fee collected from students. When the situation became really grim three years into the programme, I decided to write to all the parents of the entire body of students giving a detailed account of income and expenditure for the previous three years and asking for their support to a steep increase in tuition fee. With the approval of the Executive Council, the University increased the fee from Rs. 2500 per annum to Rs. 25,000 per annum with liberal fellowships for those who could not afford the increase. It was a pleasant surprise for me and many others that it was accepted gracefully by all without exception. Those who apprehended strike and widespread protest were silenced. Parents wrote to me saying that for the quality of education their wards were getting, they would be prepared to pay even more if another increase would become necessary! My only regret was that I could not make any enhancement on the salaries of staff who deserved much more than what they received.

Another crisis on the financial side was averted when the Ford Foundation came forward with a grant of U.S.$ 800,000 over a five year period for upgradation of library resources, clinical education programmes and faculty development initiatives. The help was quite substantial by Indian standards and came at a crucial time when the law school was finding it difficult to continue operations (i.e. 1989-94 period). When I negotiated the matter with Ford, the project Director at Delhi was Dr. Sudharsan, a Cambridge educated distinguished economist from Karnataka and who, like me, was a disciple of Justice V.R. Krishna Iyer. He took keen interest in the NLSIU project and persuaded his local boss to grant the request at least partially to the extent that was within his capacity. Later he pursued the matter at the Ford headquarters in New York at which point he quit the job to take an assignment with UNDP. His successor at Ford Foundation was Dr. Maja Daruwala who was a lawyer herself and personally appreciated the National Law School experiment. In fact, her son was a student at the National Law School who apparently gave first hand information on academic milestones happening at the law school despite financial difficulties and infra-structure problems. As luck would have it, the successor to Dr. Sudharshan did not let the project drop on the sidelines but gave it the importance it deserved by making it one of the showpieces of Ford in India. We got a total grant of 800,000 dollars in two instalments which sustained the institutional development badly needed in the initial stages of the law school.

I remember Ms. Maja Daruwala had invited me to a Conference of Senior Ford Representatives from all over the world held in Cape Town, South Africa mainly to talk about the strategic importance of Ford funding of legal education at the National Law School, Bangalore. This, according to Ford team was significant for the Foundation because of the unsatisfactory outcome of earlier Ford attempts to support legal education reforms at some universities in India in the 1960s and 70s.

Through frugal spending and efficient financial management we could generate some resources for constructing the campus facilities starting with student hostels and class rooms. With the institution of few endowments and academic Chairs sponsored by professional groups and business houses, the financial position could be further improved over the years. Several research projects and training programmes taken up by the University again helped to save some extra funds for infra-structure improvement. The University which started from nothing had assets of over ten crore of rupees when I retired from NLSIU in 1997. All this investment and expenditure over a twelve year period happened without any scandal or allegation from any quarter whatsoever. This is testimony of the honesty and integrity of all those who managed its finances during the period.

The National Law School Movement began with the Success of NLSIU

It was during this period (1995) that the Vice Chancellor of the University of Durban invited me to visit the University, study the system of legal education there and to advise on reforms in the context of the post-apartheid South Africa. I spent two weeks in Durban, lectured to students, interacted with the faculty which included a couple of Indian origin South Africans and prepared a report on possible strategies to go forward. That was the occasion when I first met Prof. McQuoid Mason who was then Dean of the Natal University Law School and a human rights activist. He later succeeded me in the Chairmanship of the Commonwealth Legal Education Association. I travelled with him to several South African law schools and inaugurated a chapter of CLEA in one of the law schools of Africa. I met the South African Chief Justice Mr. Justice Mahmood who later visited India and the National Law School. I saw the Constitution-making process in the new South Africa involving millions of citizens responding to proposals and counter-proposals where Indian experience was repeatedly referred to. I went to St. Petersberg where Gandhiji was thrown out of the train by the white colonial rulers and felt a natural affinity to the country and its people. In fact, the judiciaries of the two countries have many things in common and they face similar challenges. The legal and judicial systems are bound to bring the two countries together more closely in years to come and legal education should facilitate this process by comparative law scholarship and academic exchanges.

The first Convocation of the University was held in 1991 in the Banquet Hall of the 'Vidhan Soudha' (Seat of the state Legislature) of the State of Karnataka, had the then President of India, Dr. Shankar Dayal Sharma as its Chief Guest with Hon'ble Justice Ranganath Mishra the then Chief Justice of India, Chancellor of the University presiding over the ceremony. It was a memorable event, a turning point not only in the history of legal education but also in the lives of all those who were associated with the first law University reputed for educational and professional excellence. The profession found the products distinctly superior and sought to recruit them to legal practice. To their dismay, they found most of them picked up by multinational firms on salaries comparable to those offered for graduates of IITs and IIMs.

A Committee of judges appointed by the Chief Justice of India recommended more law schools of the National Law School Model. The All India Law Ministers' Conference wanted to have the NLS model replicated in every State. When some of the NLS products joined for higher studies in American Law Schools, there were enquiries from leading foreign law schools for exchange and joint academic programmes with NLSIU. Students from outside India including America sought admission in NLS which necessitated conduct of Admission Test in Indian embassies abroad. The University charged higher fee from foreign students which helped to improve the finances of the University. Within a span of one decade, National Law School, Bangalore became a shining star in the legal education map of the world.

At the National Law School my trusted colleague and senior partner Prof. N.L. Mitra took over as the new Director. The transition was smooth as Mitra was very much part of the institution right from the beginning and had long experience in legal education in Bengal and elsewhere. The traditions were set, the infra-structure in place and the financial position well under control, it was possible for the law school to plan expansion and seek second generation reforms. Before I relinquished office, the Chancellor appointed the Review Committee (envisaged under the NLS Act) consisting of three eminent teachers – Prof. Marc Galanter from Wisconsin University, U.S.A., Prof. William Twining from the University of London and Prof. Savitri Gunasekhere from Colombo University. They commended the success of the NLS experiment and said:

> "...The National Law School of India University has fully met the objectives of being a Centre of excellence that serves as a pace-setter for Indian legal education and a testing ground for bold experiments. Indeed, so successful has it been that it has stimulated expectations and demands that could not possibly be met by a single institution........... In the next phase, NLSIU should carefully review its activities and its role in upgrading the national system of legal education."

A Personal Tragedy Amidst Professional Success

Though I became successful in professional accomplishments, I must confess that I didn't give the time and care to my family which they deserved. This may be partly because of the faith I had in my wife. She never wanted to go for a job and thought that she had to devote all her time in the service of her husband and children. Not only did she manage the home efficiently, she also assisted the children in their studies, on many occasions after studying the lessons herself. The children, in turn, loved her more than me. It was a happy home till that fateful day, the New Year's eve of 1991. After a bitter post-operation struggle for liver complaint our daughter Devi left us to her heavenly abode at the prime age of sixteen. It was a shock which shattered the life of my wife from which she could not recover completely. My son was studying engineering in Mysore and I was in the excitement of the National Law School acquiring fame and recognition. While Devi was in hospital, I could not devote enough time with her nor could I spend time with my wife sharing the grief and pain which unfolded during the period. My colleagues led by Mr. Krishnappa, Prof. Balachandran and Mr. Chand helped us in ways in which even blood relatives often do not. In order to let her recover perhaps in the company of her son, we shifted residence to Mysore for some time. They were difficult times, painful even to recollect and impossible to narrate. My involvement with the National Law School affairs took me away from the predicament, while my wife had to live with the memories of Devi almost every day and crying to herself all the time. For some period she had to be put on treatment of a psychiatrist and a neuro-physician. A chance visit to Shri Sai Baba temple in Shirdi gave her some solace and we repeated going there. The saint Sai Baba of Shiridi remains a mystic person. Hindus believe that he is a Hindu and for Muslims he is a Muslim. Today Shirdi is the most secular shrine in India which is attracting people of all races and regions with equanimity. The serene atmosphere soothes one's soul. Life is a strange mix of joy and sorrow which no one can avoid. Faith helps us to face them with equanimity without losing our soul. There is a lot to learn from life if man cares to know. Often such a thought comes too late in life that little time is left to realize life's mission. The time may heal away the pain, but memories will remain forever.

My wife today has acquired a more wholesome attitude to life and writes poems around events which moved her. She writes them in English and Malayalam and over a hundred of them are ready. Some of her prayers were written by herself and given music also and they are being sung by many in our extended family. We hope to publish selected poems in due course. It was our decision to spend the rest of our life in Guruvayoor where we bought a flat with my savings. However, I could not get relieved of my post-retirement assignments which came one after another. Initially, she resisted and dissuaded me from taking up more and more work. When she found that I get happiness at intellectual work and that was good for my health, she adjusted herself to my schedule and let me go the way I wanted. She meanwhile cultivated her interest in birds and animals, plants and Nature and maintains a mini-Zoo around her wherever she lives. I too started developing interest in her pursuits and encouraged her in those hobbies. We manage life as it comes and await our destiny which is set by the Creator.

Recognition and Rewards from Within and Outside the Country

Meanwhile, the news about the success of the five year integrated LL.B. programme and the appropriateness of the model of its organization at the National Law School in Bangalore travelled far and wide mainly through those who graduated from NLSIU and migrated to other jurisdictions. I was invited as a Consultant by the Asian Development Bank to advise reforming legal education in Bangladesh. A young American law teacher (Prof. Jayanth Krishnan) came down to study the miracle, interviewed me and others and wrote a long article on the National Law School phenomenon in the American Journal of Legal Education (2007). The Chief Justices' Committee appointed by the Chief Justice of India (on legal education) and the All India Law Ministers' Conference recommended the replication of the National Law School model in every state. I got several invitations to assist State Governments to set up similar law schools in their respective States. In fact, one such in West Bengal I myself went to set up on the request of the then Chief Minister of the State, Mr. Jyoti Basu. I suddenly became an acknowledged reformer and a sort of rebel among legal academics.

Rewards and recognition came thick and fast. The Bar Council of India conferred a Plaque of Honour. The International Bar Association conferred "the Living Legend of Law Award". The Commonwealth Legal Education Association elected me as its President. The American Law Schools' Association invited me to address their annual conference in Florida. The Rotary Club of Bangalore conferred their prestigious award for Vocational Excellence. The Hindustan Times newspaper published from Delhi carried a news item that I was being considered by the Supreme Court Collegium for a judgeship in the apex Court which led to some embarrassing moments to me and my family. The editor of Lawyer's Collective, a legal periodical from Mumbai, even commented editorially that "the gain to the judiciary is a loss to the legal academia". I had to avoid friends and relatives for sometime to escape further embarrassment of news reports about which I had no personal information at all.

The successes of NLS experiment prompted the other State governments to start NLS model law schools in different States such as National Law Institute University, Bhopal under the leadership of Prof. V. S. Rekhi my former colleague and best friend who had laid strong academic foundations in Bhopal. Today there are more than 14 National Law Schools in India started by different State Governments.

Even some private universities are also emulating the model of NLS and giving stiff competition to the National Law Schools. Of course, for more than a billion population there is a need for more such schools.

With a sense of fulfillment I decided to withdraw on my attaining the age of 62 (age of retirement under the then prevailing NLS Statute) to settle in my hometown in Trivandrum. I took voluntary retirement from Delhi University as well which sanctioned me a pension of Rs. 7331 per month. Though my wife wanted to buy some property in Bangalore to settle there, I did not have enough savings to buy one and the only option was to return to our ancestral home in Trivandrum. However, before we could settle there, the Central Government appointed me as a Member of the Law Commission of India.

My experience as an educational administrator says that ordinary people can make big contributions in building great institutions. It has been my good fortune in life to have had the association of large number of ordinary people who extended their unqualified co-operation in fulfilling the mission I undertook in Delhi, Pondicherry, Bangalore, Kolkatta and Bhopal. This applied both to academic and administrative staff many of whom I myself selected without knowing much of their antecedents. Though everyone has contributed, I wish to re-call some of these colleagues who are fine human beings and still keep contact with me long after I left the job in those places.

Some Excellent Colleagues I came across at Bangalore

Mr. R. Krishnappa is a learned man of unimpeachable integrity, amiable manners and excellent moral character, the type of whom are seldom found in modern urban societies. He retired as Registrar of one of the oldest Agricultural Universities in the country and joined me as Registrar of National Law School, Bangalore on a meager salary. He was rich enough not to be bothered by the size of remuneration. He drove his Ambassador car himself to the law school from his house in *Indra Nagar* and carried his lunch which he often shared with me. The well-dressed man I have ever come across, he was always coming to law school in three piece suit and tie. He had a solution to every problem and willingly shared my burden and executed the job with sincerity and perfection. Everybody respected him and no one had a complaint against him. All the persons he brought in the administration also proved to be valuable asset to the University in terms of integrity, sincerity and productivity.

All the twelve years we were together in NLSIU, Bangalore there was never a scandal or strike even when we were mobilizing and spending lots of money for developing campus infra-structure. In retrospect, I wonder how I could have accomplished what I did in Bangalore, without the support and advice of Shri Krishnappa who was indeed not just a Registrar, but an elder brother to me. Whenever I go to Bangalore I try to meet him to pay my respects and admiration to the man who worked resolutely and silently in the making of a great institution.

Three other members of the staff in my team at Bangalore deserve to be mentioned for their selfless services in the making of the National Law School. Mr. Subramaniam, the Assistant Registrar is a rare combination of professional competence, unlimited tolerance and capacity to take everybody along in accomplishing the tasks assigned. Professor N.L. Mitra, my efficient and tireless colleague is not only a good teacher, but an able administrator to whom I could turn for advice to overcome difficult situations both on academic and administrative matters. Both of them rose up to great positions when they left the National Law School and acquitted themselves with distinction. Another colleague totally devoted and highly disciplined has been Prof. M.K. Balachandran for whom NLS was a 24 X 7 task. He left to become the Head of the Amity Law School in Delhi when I retired. There are several others like Prof. M.P. Padmanabha Pillai, N.S. Gopalakrishnan, Jaya Govind, Vijaya Kumar, S.V. Joga Rao, Asha Bajpai and V. Nagraj who sacrificed a great deal and worked assiduously to make the National Law School an institution to reckon with. I owe a great deal to all of them.

One other person I remember with affection and admiration is Mr. Chand Mohammed who joined me as a driver of the University vehicle but discharged the functions of messenger, guard, sweeper etc. He was always ready to undertake any job in the service of the University irrespective of whether it was day or night or working day or holiday. Chand Bhai as he was lovingly addressed by staff and students alike gave his everything to the University and, in the process, contacted some deadly disease. It was a shock to me when I heard last year that he passed away at the untimely age of 50. He was like a member of my family and accompanied me and my wife to every temple we went, although he was a devout Muslim himself. My self and my wife went to see his ailing mother in the house which Chand built with his meager earning in the suburbs of Bangalore. May his soul rest in peace.

An Award to Cherish for a Life-time

In the Ninth Convocation of the University in 2001, the Governing Council of NLSIU resolved to honour me with a Doctorate in Law and gave a Citation acknowledging my services to legal education in glorious terms. It is reproduced here:

Citation read on conferment of LL.D. (Honoris Causa) on 29-09-2001 at IX Convocation of National Law School of India University, Bangalore by the Chief Justice of India (Chancellor of the University)

"Of the many stalwarts of independent India who turned their attention to the vexatious problem of improving the quality of legal education in India, one stands out for his clarity of vision, scholarship, leadership qualities and the determination, perseverance and ability to translate ideas into reality. Revolutionising Indian legal education has been the life's mission of this true *karma yogi* who achieved what was widely considered an impossible task-establishing an institution of excellence in Indian legal education. Dr. Neelakanta Ramakrishna Madhava Menon single handedly brought fundamental change in Indian legal education and established a model that is today sought to be emulated across our country and in several other countries. Now in fifteenth successful year of its existence, the National Law School of India University, Bangalore, is a standing testimony to his vision, courage, determination and achievement.

Professor Menon took his Bachelor's Degree in Science from Kerala University in 1953, followed by a Law Degree from the same University. Professor Menon then moved to Punjab University where he was conferred a Masters Degree in Political Science in 1960. Professor Menon thereafter completed a Masters Degree in Criminal Law from Aligarh Muslim University, with distinction in all subjects. He was awarded the University Gold Medal in Criminal Law. In 1968, Professor Menon completed his doctoral studies from Aligarh University in the area of economic crimes and became the first recipient of the Ph.D. degree from Aligarh Muslim University.

Professor Menon started his chosen vocation as a law teacher in 1962, even as he was pursuing his higher studies. He rose to become Professor in the Faculty of Law, University of Delhi. During his career in Delhi University, he had a decisive influence on the academic work of the Faculty of Law, pushing it towards a greater orientation to the problems of the poor and downtrodden. The fellowships of the American Council of Learned Societies and Columbia University soon followed. Professor Menon pioneered clinical legal education in India while a member of the Faculty of Law of Delhi University. He also pioneered work on law and poverty and was a leader of the legal aid movement. During highly successful stints as Principal,

Government Law College, Pondicherry, and Dean, Faculty of Law, Annamalai University, Dr. Menon deepened his reputation as a far-sighted scholar, inspiring teacher and able administrator. As a teacher, Professor Menon inspired many generations of students, several of whom have risen to positions of national prominence. All his students gratefully acknowledge the gift of education that he has bequeathed to them. Professor Menon's active association with the Bar Council of India resulted in the Bar Council reinforcing its work in the cause of improving legal education. Professor Menon catalyzed a unique partnership between the judiciary, the bar and legal academia which has had a crucial influence in improving legal education in the country.

Academicians are often associated with an ivory tower existence, far moved from reality. But no ivory tower was strong enough to hold Dr. Menon prisoner. His keen social conscience and his active commitment to social justice and human rights ensured that his academic work was always closely connected to social realities and the law in operation. Professor Menon's academic work characterizes him as a social activist fighting for social justice through legal activism. Professor Menon's contribution to "Social Justice and Legal Process" on behalf of the Indian Social Science Academy in 1985 is the manifesto of his programme in this regard.

The best thing that could have happened to legal education in India was the appointment of Professor Menon as the founder Director of the National Law School of India University at Bangalore. There were quite a few supporters for this project but Professor Menon was the only one willing to shoulder the enormous responsibilities involved in this regard. Professor Menon set to work from day one, bringing together a little known but dedicated faculty and a group of motivated and committed students selected on the basis of merit from all over India through an unprecedented national admission test. Starting from scratch, with precious little government funding to fall back upon, Professor Menon and his team established an educational institution that has won acclaim in India and across the world. At NLSIU, Professor Menon mainstreamed the five-year undergraduate law program and brought innovative approaches to the teaching of law.

Given his accomplishments, he was naturally called upon to shoulder many other important responsibilities including that of Member, Law Commission of India. The Government of West

Bengal sought him out to head the West Bengal National University of Juridical Science, Calcutta, where he serves today as Vice Chancellor.

Professor Menon is a prolific writer, editor and scholar of legal literature. Throughout his career, he has published and disseminated legal knowledge addressing not only legal academia, the Bar and the Bench, but also non-law audiences. It is in recognition of his magnificent academic contributions that he was awarded the plaque of honour by the Bar Council of India in 1990 and the Living Legend of Law Award in 1994 by the International Bar Association. Professor Menon is today universally accepted – in India and worldwide – as the unquestioned leader of Indian legal education.

At a personal level, we know Professor Menon for his spartan habits and extreme simplicity, uncompromising honesty and integrity, endless ability for hard work and, above all, an infinite capacity to rise up to challenges. He is a born leader, an uncompromising taskmaster and a true friend.

It is but rarely that a University has the opportunity not only to honour a great scholar, a great leader, but also the very individual to whom it owes its existence and success; whose vision, courage and sacrifice lie at the core of its identity. Today, we are indeed fortunate to have such an opportunity. We honour today not only the father of modern Indian legal education; we also record our deepest gratitude to our own founding father for his selfless dedication and hard work in the service of our beloved institution.

On the occasion of the IXth Convocation of this institution that bears the indelible stamp of his stewardship, the National Law School of India University has immense pride and joy in conferring on Professor Dr. Neelakanta Ramakrishna Madhava Menon the Degree of Doctor of Laws (LL.D.) (Honoris Causa)

Dr. G. Mohan Gopal
Director, NLSIU

Dr. Justice A.S. Anand
Chief Justice of India and Visitor
National Law School of India University

An Aborted Attempt in setting up a National Law School in Kerala

I may be accused of forgetting my own State if I do not narrate an aborted attempt made in 1994 for setting up the second National Law School in the country in Kerala. Mr. K.K. Venugopal, Senior Advocate had an idea of investing a huge amount on a law university set up in the name of his distinguished father and renowned Constitutional lawyer, the late Mr. M.K. Nambyar. He consulted me and I encouraged him to establish it in Kerala. A legislation was prepared at the instance of the then Chief Minister Mr. A.K. Antony which could not be passed by the Kerala Assembly because of early announcement of State elections. When the new Government under Chief Ministership of Mr. Nayanar took office, both of us went to meet him with the proposal. He was favourably inclined. Mr. Venugopal handed over to the Chief Minister a bank draft for Rs. 2.5 crores as the seed money to get the institution started which the latter accepted. Things moved quickly and with the Chief Secretary we inspected a site near Kalady for the possible location of the University. We met Mr. Laurie Baker, the renowned architect of Kerala, to get a unique design for the campus and he welcomed the idea. We left with the impression that the Second National Law School would come up in Kerala and I would be involved in setting it up. It suited me also as I was planning to settle in Kerala on my relinquishing office from NLSIU, Bangalore taking voluntary retirement from my parent University in Delhi. The media carried reports on the forthcoming M.K. Nambyar Law University as a model in public-private partnership in higher education. Nothing happened since then and I heard that after almost a year, the advance of Rs. 2.5 crores was returned to Mr. Venugopal who later invested the amount to create an M.K. Nambyar SAARC Law Centre at the NALSAR campus in Hyderabad.

Years later in 2008, another Communist Government in Kerala requested me to Chair a Committee to recommend legal education reforms in the State which I am presently involved in. I owe a debt to Kerala which gave me my basic education in Law and I felt more than happy when an occasion was provided by the present Government in the State. I hope to submit my report in July 2009.

Establishment of Global Alliance for Justice Education

An informal meeting during American Association of Law Schools' Conference in early 1996 in Miami, USA led to a gathering of teachers, lawyers, judges and activists in Sydney, Australia in September 1996 with a common agenda for the creation of an international organization for the promotion of socially relevant legal education. This idea transformed itself in to Global Alliance for Justice Education (GAJE) in 1999. The inaugural conference was held at Thiruvanantapuram at my instance and I became a founder Member of this world wide movement for transforming legal education into justice education. The conference was attended by 125 delegates from 20 countries and the primary character of organization was relating justice and community involvement in every aspect of legal education. Workshops were conducted to address theoretical and practical issues of how justice dimension of legal education can be practically achieved. Since its first conference in India in 1999 GAJE has been conducting international Conferences and worldwide meetings on justice education regularly in different parts of the world including South Africa (2001), Poland (2004), Argentina (2006) and Philippines (2008) with increasing participation of delegates from more than 50 countries.

The GAJE Mission Statement makes its' objectives clear. It says, GAJE is GLOBAL, seeking to involve persons from as many countries in the world as possible, avoiding domination by any single country, and especially committed to meaningful participation from less affluent countries, institutions, and organizations. GAJE is an ALLIANCE of persons committed to achieving justice through legal education. Clinical education of law students is a key component of justice education, but this organization also works to advance other forms of socially relevant education, which includes education to practicing lawyers, judges, non-governmental organizations and the lay public.

To continuously endeavour to achieve excellence in one's chosen field is now a fundamental duty of every citizen. For me legal education reform became a passion and life's mission. Despite the setbacks and criticisms I have encountered from some senior colleagues and a section of advocates, I took it upon myself the impossible task of changing the way law was practised in India. My book on the legal profession in Tamilnadu (1981) had alienated a section of the bar that looked at my activities with suspicion and disbelief. The success of the National Law School generated professional jealousy in certain educational circles and in places where I had nothing to do any way.

News about the success of the five year integrated LL.B. programme and the appropriateness of the model of its organization at the National Law School in Bangalore travelled far and wide mainly through those who graduated from NLSIU and migrated to other jurisdictions. I got several invitations to assist State Governments to set up similar law schools in their respective States. In fact, one such in West Bengal I myself went to set up on the request of the then Chief Minister of the State, Mr. Jyoti Basu.

Hesitant Venture to Reform Legal Education in West Bengal

My appearance in the legal education scene in West Bengal was not taken kindly by a section of the academic legal community there despite the fact that I was invited by no less a person than the then Chief Minister of the State, the highly respected Mr. Jyoti Basu. I was neither a Bengali nor a member of the communist party to be preferred for the job. People involved in legal education in Bengal were intrigued at my invitation and perhaps hoped that I would give up and leave sooner than later. In fact, the whole thing happened rather by accident than by plan. An unusual call from the Chief Minister's office set the ball rolling. The most revered Mr. Jyoti Basu came on the line, recalled his visit two years ago to the National Law School, Bangalore and asked me to help West Bengal set up a similar institution in Kolkata. My reply was that I would certainly give whatever help I could extend from Trivandrum where we have decided to settle in retirement. I was at that time a part-time Member of the Law Commission of India also. He gave the phone to his Law Minister who wanted me to frame a blue print and a Statute for setting up the law school. I did it in a fortnight and sent the draft to the Law Minister. Within days I got a call again to visit Kolkata to discuss the matter. In a meeting at Kolkata Raj Bhavan, besides the Governor who was at that time the Chief Justice of the High Court, Mr. Jyoti Basu with his Cabinet Colleagues were present. Several details including fee structure and the draft Statute which I sent earlier were discussed. In the next few weeks I was informed that the Law University Bill was promulgated as an Ordinance and the Government resolved to invite me as its first Vice Chancellor. The Chief Minister again talked to me and persuaded me to go to Kolkata. He talked to my wife and said that life would be as pleasant there as in Trivandrum and I would face no difficulty in organizing the law school there. Coming from a Senior Statesman and a revered leader who is himself a barrister, I could not decline the invitation though it was something I was reluctant to take up after refusing to continue in Bangalore for another term. In fact, later the Law Minister told me that the Chief Justice of India (Dr. Justice A.S. Anand) had told him that Prof. Menon would not take up the job as he declined it when he was asked to continue for another term in Bangalore. When destiny dictates, man is helpless. My Kolkata assignment was such a sudden and unexpected event which upset my retirement plans in my home State.

In consultation with my wife, I decided not to accept any salary for my position as Vice Chancellor. I would serve in an honorary capacity so that I could honorably quit if things got too difficult for me or my independence of action was subverted. I also took extra care to see that nothing was done contrary to the norms and procedures prescribed under Statutes of the University. The support of the Government of West Bengal and more particularly of the Chief Minister and Law Minister made my task easier than expected and I must record my unqualified appreciation and gratitude to them.

By "juridical sciences" we mean the entire range of knowledge in the realm of physical, natural or the social sciences as they impact on society. "Justice" is perceived not just as a scheme based on a set of rights and duties, but as a relational experience to be structured according to societal values and to be measured in terms of respect for human rights and justice for all.

There are several ways in which the law school of the future can be conceived. One possibility is to look at the society around, identify the major problems which contribute to injustices and address the role of law, lawyers and courts in containing them. This is the needs-assessment and problem-solving approach.

A second approach is to articulate the goals of law education from the Constitution and from accumulated experience in legal scholarship and relate them to the perceived functions of a justice-oriented law school. This is the goal-oriented, trial-and-error approach. Yet another approach could be to look at what is being done in some of the reputed law schools around the world and pick those aspects appealing to one's perception of "Justice Education" and structure a curriculum and an institutional framework for the job in hand.

Each one has its merits and demerits. Of course, there are situational constraints which impinge not only on the choice of the model but also the extent to which it can be executed.

I went alone to Kolkata in May 1999 as there was no institution to administer or students to teach and the work involved was running around to meet concerned people and putting together basic infra-structural requirements to begin with. The Assembly passed the West Bengal National University of Juridical Sciences Act, 1999 and notified it in the Gazette with another notification announcing Prof. Menon as its first Vice Chancellor. The Chief Justice of India was made the Chancellor of the University. The Governing Body included representatives from the Bar Council, the Judiciary, the State Government (Law, Finance and Education), the U.G.C. and the Academia. I had got the institutional autonomy I asked for which was something unprecedented in higher education in West Bengal. At the instance of the Chief Minister, a newly constructed building Aranya Bhavan at Salt Lake belonging to the Forest Department was allotted as temporary home of NUJS. I got busy with selection of faculty, assembling the necessary furniture, locating accommodation for students and faculty, selecting few essential administrative staff and finding a place for me to live in somewhere near the campus. To extract funds from Government for all these and more was a stupendous task and I became a daily visitor to Writer's Building, the Secretariat of the Government of West Bengal. Conversing in English and Hindi, I became friendly with people in the Writer's Building. They took me as an outsider perhaps setting up an industry in Kolkata! Some of them in the Writers Building requested me to accommodate their educated unemployed children in my enterprise. I was burdened with a few CVs also in the process. What struck me most was an encounter with a security guard in white uniform at the entrance of the Writer's Building telling me in one of my visits that he holds an LL.M. Degree and will be happy to join as a Lecturer in the new University if the position was offered to him.

Changing the Rules of Business of the Government of West Bengal, the Judicial Department (instead of the Education Department) was given the administrative charge of the University. I found the Hon'ble Law Minister Mr. Nisith Adhikary very humble, understanding and co-operative willing to do whatever I sought, of course, subject to the limitations of Government procedures. Together we met all concerned Ministers repeatedly to mobilize the requisite resources and support systems. Our object was to get the admission done and teaching started at the shortest possible time in any case within one year of the Notification establishing the University.

The initial problem was land and that too in or around the city. An institute for professional studies could not be far away from the centre of professional activity, the Courts and law chambers. Calcutta city had little land to offer. We had to scale down substantially from our demand for 35 acres. During the negotiations with the Government we were told that we would be given sufficient land if we locate the campus 40 kms away from the city on the way to Kalyani, which we could not agree. At the instance of the Hon'ble Law Minister, Mr. Nisith Adhikari, we were shown two plots in Salt Lake, one measuring 5 acres and another half its size nearby. I bargained for both but finally settled for a bigger unit on a prime location on the eastern bypass road. In getting possession of the land we had to wait for several months, cross many bureaucratic hurdles, part with substantial money (Rs. 30 lakhs) and settle for only 4.7 acres which was all what was left at the site, apparently due to illegal encroachment by some unfriendly neighbour.

In one of my early visits to Kolkata early 1999, I was introduced by the then Governor of the State to a solemn looking tall man, Mr. Subimal Ghosh, chief of the firm of architects, Ghosh, Bose & Associates. I had several meetings with him discussing my dream of a centre for excellence in legal studies. I asked him whether he could dream with me and develop an idea of a structure which would be a masterpiece, a landmark in the city while fulfilling all the needs of a dynamic campus of higher learning. He asked me about the land. I said I did not yet have it. He enquired about the money available and its source. I replied the quantum was not known and the source was the West Bengal Government. He was not impressed or at least I felt so. We parted to meet again on some future date when land and money were available. However, he seemed to have been taken by my daring to initiate talks with a leading architect with neither land nor money in hand. He must have been surprised when I telephoned him few months later to say that land would be available very soon. When I told him the location in Salt Lake, he felt enthused, but when I informed him about the size of the land, he wondered whether it would at all be sufficient for a University of my conception. Beggars could not be choosers! The Law Minister alone knew how many battles he had to fight to get even this much land for a University which was at that time still on paper only.

Mr. Subimal Ghosh and his colleagues got into the act any way. We did not even discuss the terms, nor was he engaged formally as the official architects at that point of time. He brought alternate plans; we discussed again the advantages and disadvantages. My demands increased; he reminded me of the constraints of land and money. We finally settled that there was no alternative except to build skywards. He told me, taking account of the sand condition in Salt Lake and the probable height of the construction, lots of pile work would have to be undertaken which would increase the costs. He gave an estimate of over 40 crores of rupees, a sum I could not even dream to command. I told him nothing exceeding 20 crores would be available and that too little uncertain. He was quick to feed me with alternate plans and drawings every time I told him of a new idea. Soon it dawned on us that without assurance of a steady flow of cash, it was foolish to start construction of even the foundation. The Law and Finance Ministers, both members of NUJS Executive Council, enthusiastically assured me that Government would fund the project over a period of time. Perhaps, taking the convention in Government constructions, the Ministers would have thought that I was talking of a ten year project. They would have presumed that to find 20 crores over 10 years would be within the range of possibility in Government finances. My idea on the other hand was a two year venture. 20 crores in 2 years ? impossible, even for Central Government, said my friends in the Writers' Building!

I took the plans for a new campus to the Executive Council which approved it with minor changes. They wanted more single rooms in the hostel as the students should be given more comforts if they were to put in their best to legal studies. The Council desired to have the library, auditorium and seminar halls to be air-conditioned to beat sultry weather of Kolkata summer and to let uninterrupted academic activity. Excellent ideas for a center of excellence. What about the money? Should I go for finding the builders with no provision or a token provision only in the budget? It was then decided that we would go for the pile work for the time being for which Government grant would be forthcoming over a period of one or two years. In other words, the thinking in 2000 was that the foundation would be readied by 2003 by which time plans for mobilization of more funds would be sorted out.

The cost of pile work was estimated at Rs. 4 crores. If mobilization of rupees 4 crores was a three year task, then, of course, the 20 crore complex would be completed in 10 to 15 years only. I was depressed. I might not live that long; in any case my term as V.C. would end by the time the pile work was completed and the contractor fully paid up. Meanwhile, fresh admission of students would have to be suspended because of lack of space in 'Aranya Bhavan', where we were located temporarily in two floors, courtesy, the then Chief Minister, Mr. Jyoti Basu.

The mobilization of necessary fund was an adventure at Kolkota. Having read in newspapers that some housing finance companies were lending money for construction, I went to Delhi to meet the M.D. of one such company, HUDCO. When I wrote him seeking an appointment and conveying the object, to my pleasant surprise, he replied promptly by fax not only welcoming me but suggesting that HUDCO would be pleased to consider financing a "prestigious project like NUJS Campus". When I later met him in Delhi, I found him to be a fellow Keralite fairly knowledgeable about what I did for legal education at the National Law School, Bangalore. Without much persuasion I could get him committed for a 20 crore loan provided I secured a Government guarantee for prompt repayment of installments over a 15 year period. The Executive Council promptly approved the loan proposal. I did not realize that a promise of loan even from the M.D. of HUDCO would not enable me to have possession of the money in reasonable time! Paper work is unbelievable. Babus would treat the applicants as beggars and would suspect every statement you make and would question why a law college would need so much money at all. They queried again and again whether the Government was at all serious of what they promised. Between HUDCO regional office and the Writers' Building we spent the next few months with diminishing hopes and increasing frustration. Questions were asked why the plans were so made and suggestions were made that unless the whole thing was re-done as they advised, the request might not even be forwarded to the head office!

After a long wait (which I understood was too short from the point of view of the establishment) I made a second visit to the M.D. at Delhi and explained my predicament. He directed me to another senior officer in charge of finances who was very understanding and amiable. He promised to talk to the Kolkata regional office and speed up the process. He wanted me to give another month before I would call on him again. As luck would have it, things worked with greater speed and I was informed that the HUDCO Board had sanctioned the loan and I would be able to draw the first installment if I completed the formalities of the agreement. A key factor of the agreement was the Government guarantee. With the best efforts of the Hon'ble Law Minister, the Cabinet approved the loan and the guarantee letter was eventually issued. Nothing doing, said HUDCO. The language had to be different. Government should write that the successive budgets would provide the money for repayment. On our plea, Government issued a modified order which again did not satisfy the creditors. With anger and frustration, I decided to meet the M.D. again who himself showed some amount of displeasure at the conduct of his own officials. He asked me to stay back in Delhi and meet him again after a couple of days. Luck worked again and when I went back to HUDCO office, a cheque for Rs. 3.5 crores being the first installment of the loan was waiting for me. I was overjoyed, telephoned my office in Kolkata of what happened and asked them to expedite the construction contract papers.

The exemplary dynamism and leadership which the members of the Executive Council bestowed on this project helped it to be completed in a record time of 22 months. We did the routine and presented papers to the Council. Judges of the highest court of the land who adorn the NUJS bodies took personal interest in probing the strengths and weaknesses of each proposal, discussing with the builders and contractors directly for the works in respect of quality, cost and time and deciding expeditiously the action to be taken and the terms of the contracts to be finalized. In this regard, the contribution of Hon'ble Mr. Justice B.N. Kirpal who later became the Chancellor of the University in the capacity of the Chief Justice of India had to be acknowledged with eternal gratitude by every member of the NUJS Family.

Side by side with the construction activity, the University prepared its academic programmes, selected the core faculty and staff, set up the library and announced the admission for the five year B.A., LL.B. (Hons) course. The response was indeed amazing and the University had no difficulty in selecting 80 outstanding students from all over the country and abroad promising a good start to academic activities. Following the principle adopted by me in Bangalore, the administrative staff was kept to the minimum and most of the tasks of cleaning, security, transport and even fee collection was outsourced. Corporation Bank set up its branch in the campus and undertook much of the financial transactions on behalf of the University. The University and its work culture attracted attention of the intelligentia from within Kolkata and outside. A series of national and international conferences, student activities including moot court, legal aid and a journal as well as a couple of large research projects supported by the Ford Foundation and World Bank put the University in the legal education map of India in a short span of 2 to 3 years. The School of Criminal Justice of NUJS under my responsibility started a major research project of compiling data and publishing status report on crime and criminal justice in each and every state of India. Over 20 criminal justice status reports were commercially published in less than 3 years building a country-wide network of active players of criminal justice administration as intellectual partners of NUJS. The University suddenly became a major player in criminal justice education, training and research in the country. Prof. D. Banerjea, an experienced judge, scholar and trainer directed the activities of the School of Criminal Justice. My decade old experience in NLS, Bangalore had come handy in launching the academic programmes in Calcutta (now Kolkota).

Some Events to Remember in Kolkata Project

I must admit that I found the Kolkata people generally supportive of scholarly pursuits. The parents of students took great interest in the academic activities of the University and the performance of their wards. I was invited to Chair the Governing Board of the prestigious Indian Statistical Institute (ISI) for a two year period succeeding Reserve Bank Governor, Dr. Bimal Jalan. I used the opportunity to promote law and economics scholarship in both the institutions, NUJS and ISI. Legal literacy classes were started in a number of colleges in the city under the sponsorship of NUJS Legal Services Clinic. The University became a centre of attraction for scholars and the media projected the success story to the people within and outside West Bengal.

During the period of my Vice-Chancellorship of NUJS a leading law firm in Delhi approached me to give an opinion on the law of damages in torts in India for supporting litigation in New York against a Sports TV Channel. Taking some research assistance from students I prepared a 40 page brief which the firm approved and sent to New York. To my pleasant surprise three months later, I received a cheque of Rs. three

Lakhs as my consultation fee from the law firm. It was for the first time I received a consultation fee of that kind and I was in doubt whether I deserve such a big amount. After all, the students also worked to prepare the brief. After much reflection, I decided to donate the entire amount as an endowment to NUJS to promote teaching and research on Sports Laws/Media Law in the University. I was delighted to note that the University readily instituted an endowment and encouraged sports and media law activities perhaps for the first time in India.

Another unique experience I had with the students and faculty of NUJS deserve mentioning here. In 2000 Gujarat was struck by a-severe earthquake causing terrible death and destruction in an unprecedented scale. Seeing the images of the devastation on the TV screen and moved by the suffering of the people, few of us discussed as to what the legal community could possibly do in such situation. Several ideas were discussed and few of us from NUJS decided to take a team to Kutch to assist the victims using our knowledge of law and administration. There were a dozen students and a couple of faculty members with me. My wife accompanied the team. We sought the assistance of the Gujarat Legal Services Authority and we got liberal assistance from Hon'ble Justice J.N. Bhat, the then Chairman and Dr. Joshi, the then Secretary of Gujarat Legal Services Authority. We stayed in Kutch for almost a week, did whatever we could do to mitigate the suffering and collected lot of data on the legal services needs of the victims which included lots of women and children. On return to Ahmedabad we submitted our report to the Legal Aid Authority as well as the Chief Justice of the High Court who had a PIL on the subject before him. Both appreciated our effort and made use of our suggestions in ordering reliefs and services accordingly on the PIL pending before it. From my point of view it was a great learning experience on law in social context, a realization of the poverty of law or the limits of it and the need for lawyers to be involved in organizing legal relief operations after large scale disasters. We conducted a series of meetings back in Kolkata and helped the State Government on mounting a disaster management plan in times of floods, a perennial problem in West Bengal.

The students won many laurels in academic pursuits. A team from NUJS went to Vienna in 2002 to participate in the International Moot on Commercial Arbitration and won the first prize defeating the American contestants in the final round. I got further proof to argue that given guidance and motivation, our students can do better than others in legal education as well.

I got the satisfaction that I could by and large accomplish the mandate given to me by the West Bengal Government within four years of the conception of a centre of excellence in legal studies in the eastern metropolis. The campus infra-structure was completed and four batches of students were performing well in studies, research and co-curricular activities. In another year I would have graduated the first batch of students from NUJS and my five year tenure would have been completed. But before I could do so the Chief Justice of India (Justice B.N. Kirpal) who was also the Chancellor of NUJS wanted me to find my successor and move to Bhopal to set up the National Judicial Academy, an institution for training judges of the higher judiciary functioning under the direct supervision of the Supreme Court. I tried to delay my departure for almost an year; but finally on his insistence I decided to leave NUJS by September 2003. On the request of the State Law Minister to find my successor in office, I talked to my good friend Dr. B.S. Chimni of Jawaharlal Nehru University who agreed to go to NUJS to continue with the unfinished job. He was eventually appointed as my successor Vice Chancellor at NUJS.

Again in Calcutta some excellent colleagues helped to build a great institution there. I was again blessed with a set of people who, as the saying goes, considered "Work as Worship". Again, four persons stand out whom I cannot afford to miss in my memoirs. Prof. Gangotri Chakravarty is a person who can take any responsibility and complete it with finesse and tact. At the National University of Juridical Sciences she was not only a Professor of Law, but also the Registrar, the Warden of the hostel and a sort of public relations officer for the law school. For me, a stranger to Bengal, her help and advice were essential to get my mission completed in record time. When I learnt that at home she had to look after her ailing parents also, my respect and admiration for her naturally grew manifold. As a teacher also she excelled and won appreciation from the entire student body.

Another colleague whom I had invited to join NUJS was Dr. Bhavani Prasad Panda, a scholar who never complained about the volume of work. He was always energetic, enthusiastic and cheerful. I made him in charge of Boys Hostel and Examinations along with regular academic assignments. Soon he became very popular among students. He is an asset to any institution.

Mr. Kanunjno came from the National Human Rights Commission as Accounts Officer of the University with rich credentials from Justices M.N. Venkatachaliah and V.S. Malimath. He proved to be an asset to the infant University with his diligence, efficiency and sincerity of purpose. His services were not confined to the finance and accounting. He involved himself in the academic and administrative activities and worked in the team in building a dream institution of higher learning.

Nowadays he is working as Finance Officer of a Central University in Assam; yet he keeps visiting NUJS and extends whatever help the authorities wanted as if it is his own institution. That is the spirit which makes great institutions possible.

Ali is a young man who joined me as a peon in the University. Like Chand in Bangalore, Ali worked not only as a messenger but a security guard, a despatch clerk, a health assistant etc. A man of complete honesty and integrity he has been a wonderful colleague and a helpful friend. I wanted to take him to Bhopal and give him a better position in the National Judicial Academy. However, he could not move out of Kolkata because of family circumstances. I wish to record my debt of gratitude to all these wonderful Colleagues, men and women who are indeed great human beings and institution-builders in their own right.

How I became a Teacher in China

In early 2000 while I was setting up the National University of Juridical Sciences at Kolkata, I got a call from the Ford Foundation in Delhi asking me whether I could respond to a request from their counterpart in Beijing for some assistance regarding legal education. I was intrigued what China had to get from me and that too in legal education. The request was about giving permission to translate and publish one of my books on Clinical Legal Education published by Eastern Book Co. a-decade ago. I agreed to the request without any hesitation and asked them to contact the publishers who held the copyright regarding royalty payment etc. I was greatly pleased that the Chinese law teachers found the book worthy of translation when there are hundreds of books on the subject available mainly from American authors.

The book was translated into Chinese by two law teachers of that country and I was invited to release the Chinese edition the very next year. The occasion was the Chinese Law Teachers' Conference in the City of Hunan. I went with my wife, released the book and congratulated the teachers who did the translation. I was pleasantly surprised at the importance China was giving to set up law schools, train law teachers and modernize the legal system at break-neck speed. Nearly six hundred law teachers were present at the conference where communication was difficult because of language problems. However, several teachers told me that they were following my book in organizing clinical legal education in their respective law schools. I invited them to visit India and spend time with law schools in this country which idea they liked very much. They wanted to pick up some English language competence before they planned to visit India.

On return, I felt that India would have to pay a heavy price for neglect of China in its educational campuses. It is our big neighbour with which we have increasing trade and diplomatic relations. We know very little of Chinese legal system and whatever we know of it is what was written by western writers, largely perceived from their own experience. It is necessary for selected Indian Law Schools to set up Chairs on Chinese law, initiate comparative law scholarship, develop exchange programmes and promote joint research projects. If clinical legal education is to be the window through which these contacts can develop, let it be. We have now greater expertise to share and learn from experiments in Chinese law schools. I hope some National Law Schools will take the initiative in this regard.

Prospects for Better Legal Education

In India we have many divisive forces on the basis of caste, creed, religion and region. Unfortunately, education also reflects these divisive forces. In the beginning my enthusiasm was to contribute for the improvement of legal education with common standards in all law schools and colleges by introducing integrated five year law programme replacing the three years course. Today legal education is organized basically in three streams. The National Law Schools offering the best standards but only for the privileged few. The University law colleges are available to the next best. Finally, the private law colleges with varying degrees of quality are available for the rest. There are good students and good teachers every where and the academic atmosphere and financial support are making the difference in the outcome. It is unfortunate that even in primary and school education we have a differentiated system which denies equal opportunity for weaker sections to access the best of education. The advent of privatization is further aggravating the situation and 'good education' tend to become a commodity traded in the educational market place! I wish despite the market forces and the divisiveness in our social organization, legal education imparted by all types of law teaching institutions will improve under the impact of the National Law School Movement and the five year integrated curriculum.

Of course, no educational scheme particularly in our present context can be perfect or can last for all times. The process has to continue by innovation and experimentation. Everyone is dissatisfied in varying degrees with the prevailing state of legal education including perhaps the college managements. The reasons for dissatisfaction may be different and the perception of the problems may also vary. Selecting teachers and students with proper motivation and providing appropriate facilities and educational environment are necessary to take the reform movement forward. The NLS experiment apparently offers these prospects. The Bar Council should reduce its role and let the law schools design and implement their programmes with greater autonomy and accountability. The situation demands consideration of alternative strategies at appropriate levels. The educational experiment should not get sabotaged by vested interests that stand to gain by the continuation of *status quo*.

The twenty-first century is going to be a totally different world than most of us are familiar with or can imagine in our conventional mindset. It is difficult even to comprehend the dimensions of change and the demands of the legal profession in the next millennium. Given the prospects for trade in services, we need to produce transnational lawyers comfortable with legal systems other than their own. Given the growth of information and communication technology, we must anticipate the changing styles of advocacy and prepare the future lawyers to be proficient in managing all types of information, not just the statutes and judicial decisions. To my mind for the first time in history, the legal profession is under threat of invasion from other professions unless the profession itself changes its nature and methods of delivery of services. To be able to teach intellectual property laws or natural resources laws or to train students in negotiation and business planning, the law school of the future has to go multi-disciplinary and multi-national in its teaching programmes. This is a challenge which law schools in most Asian countries have not addressed themselves as yet !

A critical re-evaluation of our legal education programme both in terms of substantive content and methodology is required. To be able to do this, we have to have a clear vision of our objects, the challenges we face and the alternatives available to us in our respective States. The vocational role of law has come to occupy the central concern in curriculum planning and development. The Socratic and clinical methods of teaching have assumed special place in pedagogy at the law school. There has to be bilateral and multi-lateral co-operation in these matters.

Chapter IV

Legal Education to Judicial Education: Experiments at NJA, Bhopal

LEGAL EDUCATION TO JUDICIAL EDUCATION: EXPERIMENTS AT NJA, BHOPAL

Hon'ble Justice B.N. Kirpal, the then Chief Justice of India was emphatic of my shifting to Bhopal where the infra-structure development of the proposed National Judicial Academy was taking too long a time despite heavy investment. He was in a hurry to start the training programmes for judges and sounded me on the assignment in early 2002. In April 2003 while receiving Padma Shree from the then President, His Excellency Dr. A.P.J. Abdul Kalam told me that the NJA was awaiting my arrival and I should go to Bhopal at the earliest. My wife who was with me at the time was surprised at the suggestion coming from no less a person than the President of the Republic. For the first time in my life I felt elated that people at high places had great expectations from me even after my retirement from a fairly long academic career. My wife and my self felt that it was a direction which we should honour though I could claim no special expertise to develop a judicial training institution. Anyway the decision was made in Rashtrapati Bhavan in April 2003 and there was no question of looking back. I met the Chief Justice the next day and informed him that I would join Bhopal later in the year after finding a successor to hold fort at NUJS, Kolkata.

In July 2003 I went to Bhopal to study the situation there and to prepare myself for the tasks ahead. Construction work was suspended for over a year because of some dispute between the architects and the contractors. There were problems in getting regular water supply and electricity. After a round of consultations with the parties concerned, an agreement was reached and work resumed. There were two District Judges deputed by Madhya Pradesh High Court working as Registrars overseeing the construction activity of the campus which was formally inaugurated by Dr. Kalam himself few months earlier. I informed them that I would join as Director in September, 2003 and would like to start the training programmes straightaway despite the difficulties involved on infra-structure arrangements. I impressed upon the contractors the need to complete the essential works immediately to enable judges from all over the country to stay in campus and attend the training sessions. The chief architect was summoned from Bombay and was instructed to get the remaining works completed whatever be the cost and effort involved. My experience in the construction of two University campuses in Bangalore and Kolkata did give me adequate expertise to deal with architects and contractors using the carrot and stick policy. Things worked remarkably well and the essential facilities in the campus got ready by the time I formally took up the Directorship of the Academy in September, 2003.

The Campus of the National Judicial Academy is situated on the banks of the Bhopal lake on a hillock covering over 60 acres of undulating land. The architects have preserved the landscape and built a string of impressive buildings overlooking the lake on all sides. Perhaps NJA enjoyed the best of facilities expected for a training institution and could easily claim to be the topmost training centre for judges in this part of the world. This was what Chief Justices from abroad who visited the Academy recorded in their impressions.

Beginning of another Innings at Institution Building

The day when I arrived at National Judicial Academy I felt I was again all alone and the team has to be assembled afresh. My experiments and experience in legal education for more than four decades and my new assignment in preparing the judiciary for better delivery of justice made me to think afresh on what is 'justice'? Does common people have any faith in the judiciary to deliver timely justice? Whether justice is accessible to all? In view of my involvement and commitment to Global Alliance for Justice Education what kind of training I should impart to judges? What are the qualities of a good judge? What kind of programmes I have to arrange? Are the judges going to be receptive? Truly speaking I myself had no idea of "methods' of judicial training.

Indian judiciary has a glorious past and great judges like Sir Gooroodas Benererji, Sir Asutosh Mukherjee, Sir James Peacock, Sir Shah Mohammed Sulaiman, Sir Ramesh Chandra Mitter, Sir Sankaran Nair had enriched the judicial history with their invaluable services and commitment to professional excellence. In the post independence era celebrated names of Justices S.R. Das, Patanjali Sastri, B. Varadachariar, Vivin Bose, M.C. Chagla, K.Subba Rao, H.R. Khanna, V.R. Krishna Iyer and many others have given luster to the high Bench. Yet, the common man is reportedly losing faith in the judiciary due to delay and clouds of corruption which plagued administration of justice. Can education and training of judges make a difference in the scenario and bring back the glory of yester years?

Unlike the Universities where I worked before, at NJA, I had no academic colleagues to depend on or to seek assistance from for developing the training modules and designing the programmes. The Resource Persons for training were usually sitting and retired judges of the Supreme Court and High Courts who had to be identified (based on their expertise) and had to be invited to Bhopal during the days when training programmes were organized. There was hardly any person in Bhopal who could be associated with judicial training for superior court justices. My long association with the Bar Council of India Trust during 1980s and 1990s in designing and conducting continuing education programmes for advocates did give me some insights on adult learning, skills training and programme development. In that background, I ventured into judicial education and training and came up with a Programme Statement and a series of training courses varying between 3 to 15 days. The emphasis was on case management, court craft, judgement writing, and appreciation of evidence, special skills for courts of special jurisdiction, judicial ethics and arrears reduction. The structure of the course depended on whether the programme was directed at District Judges or High Court justices. In the case of the former, the structure was workshop model while in the case of the latter it was more of seminar type. In both cases the sessions were to be interactive. Materials were put together in advance and sent to participants for prior reading. They were invited to raise questions and suggest issues which they wanted the experts to particularly focus on during their presentations. It was a policy to have a panel of at least two persons in every session (a judge and a lawyer / academic / activist / professional) so that the different dimensions of the issue are brought out from diverse experience. Power point and other audio-visual aids were liberally used to save time and maximize the learning process. Care was taken to see that the training programmes gave not only knowledge and skills but promoted attitudinal changes by interrogating established patterns of perception and belief. The preparation for these programmes demanded lot of consultation and effort which led me to interact with judges at all levels, sitting and retired. I read available literature on judicial training from other countries and came in touch with some of the experienced judicial trainers mostly from USA, Canada and U.K. In fact, within two years of my work at the National Judicial Academy I was invited to be a Member of the Governing Board of the International Association of

Judicial Educators which had as its president the former Chief Justice of Israel. I was one of the few academics in the midst of a large number of distinguished judges of superior courts from among eighty four countries!

The Commonwealth Judicial Education Institute (CJEI) located in Halifax, Canada is an association of superior court justices affiliated to the Commonwealth Secretariat. Ms. Sandra Oxner, a retired judge of the Canadian Supreme Court is its President. In one of her visits to India she came to see the National Judicial Academy and got deeply impressed by its facilities and programmes. She desired to have joint programmes between NJA and CJEI and the first such venture was a Commonwealth Chief Justices' Conference to discuss issues of mutual concern. In April 2005 the Conference was organized in which judges from over thirty countries including eighteen Chief Justices participated. I had organized two regular training programmes for Indian judges during the period and utilized the services of foreign judges to address them on issues of delay and arrears in courts. It was indeed a memorable event in the early stages of NJA to have hosted the world judiciary and to project the shining image of the Indian judiciary. Judge Sandra Oxner became a regular visitor to India since then and we conducted many joint programmes for judges in Bhopal and elsewhere. I was invited as a Speaker to the Intensive Study Programme which CJEI organized every summer at Halifax (Canada) for judges from the Commonwealth countries. This association continued even after my relinquishing the job at Bhopal. The Intensive Study programme is indeed a model to be emulated by judicial educators everywhere. It is a comparative study and reflection by judges of superior courts themselves on issues and challenges of common concern to all judicial systems. Best practices are identified, analyzed and assimilated. Joint projects and exchange programmes are evolved and implemented. Fraternity among Commonwealth judges cultivated and judicial values assimilated. Judge Sandra Oxner spends her own funds besides those generated from sponsors to support the activities of CJEI. She has many friends in Indian judiciary and many Indians including me are in CJEI team of advisors and patrons. Indian High Court and Supreme Court justices do participate in the programmes organized at Halifax every year. For me an invitation every year to participate in the Intensive Study Programme at Halifax from Judge Sandra Oxner is a refreshingly welcome change particularly in my retired life.

I had occasion to attend the Conference of the International Association of Judicial Educators held in Ottawa in 2005 where I was nominated to the Board of Governors of that body. I was deeply impressed by the idea of "social context judging" popularized by the Canadian Supreme Court and the Canadian Judicial Academy which, I felt was part of Indian judicial practice as well.

I continue to be an advisor to the CJEI and am invited to visit Canada every year to participate in the Intensive Study Programme organized by the Institute for Commonwealth judges. An academician among justices of superior courts is perhaps not always welcome in this country but I found it acceptable in Canada.

I must mention in this context the recruitment of Ms. Lakshmi Vijyabalan, Research Associate from NJA to the staff of CJEI in Canada. She continues to work as an Assistant to Judge Oxner in organizing the programmes of CJEI and she has now become a sort of an expert in judicial training. Her husband Mr. Tony George who was also a Research Associate at NJA is now pursuing doctoral studies at the law school in University of Halifax. Another Research Associate who worked with me at NJA, Ms. Geeta Oberoi is now pursuing her doctoral studies at the University of Warwick, U.K. again on a subject related to judicial education and training. I persuaded these young colleagues to go abroad in the hope that when they came back they would bring comparative scholarship in judicial education and training to enrich the programmes in the judicial training academies in India.

NJA acquired a reputation in judicial education and training within a short time because of the dynamic leadership of successive Chief Justices and judges of the Indian Supreme Court and the impressive infra-structure built up in its Bhopal campus. My effort has been to promote institutionalization of judicial training for subordinate judiciary in every state. By 2008 as many as eighteen High Courts have set up State Judicial Academies and developed infra-structure to organize programmes by themselves, sometimes with the help of NJA. NJA on its part took upon itself the task of standardizing training curriculum, developing study materials and organizing training of trainers (TOT) programmes. On the publication front, NJA brought out an annual journal, a quarterly Newsletter and a series of Occasional Papers on topics of interest to the judiciary. The remaining part of construction of the campus was soon completed and regular staff appointed to carry the mission forward.

Supreme Court Justices make History : Retreat at NJA

One other significant event which happened during my tenure as the Founder Director of NJA needs to be mentioned here. This was a week long Intellectual Retreat organized for Supreme Court Justices at NJA in the summer of 2005. When I initially mooted the idea with the then Chief Justice of India, he was not sure whether his Brethren would welcome the idea. Thanks to the insight and persuasion of Hon'ble Justices Ruma Pal and Santosh Hegde, the Retreat did take place and thirteen judges of the Supreme Court including the Chief Justice of India participated and attended daily sessions organized during the week on topics related to impact of science and technology, implications of a liberalized and globalizing economy, developments in public law in different jurisdictions and management in courts. Several experts made presentations and interacted with the Supreme Court Justices for the first time in Indian judicial history. The President of India, Dr. Abdul Kalam was one of the Resource Persons who addressed and answered questions put to him by the justices.

One of the last programmes I had organized for Superior Court justices from countries outside India was for a dozen Appellate Court judges from Sri Lanka. Earlier, NJA had organized a fortnight long course for judges from Ghana. This experience led to my being invited as an expert in few judicial training programmes outside India as well. Thus my life as a law teacher for over 45 years got transformed as a judicial educator, rather unexpectedly.

I enjoyed my tenure at NJA and the Supreme Court was keen to continue my tenure even beyond the advanced age of 72 years. However, fate decided otherwise. My wife contacted an acute form of arthritis which necessitated hospitalization in Kerala. We decided to call it a day and seek permanent retirement from active service to spend time with relatives in our home town in Kerala.

The Chief Justice of India asked me to find a new Director to take over the NJA administration well before my departure. Meanwhile a Committee was constituted by the Chief Justice of India for finding my successor who contacted Dr. Mohan Gopal and made the proposal. Dr. Gopal expressed his difficulty because of family circumstances. While these discussions were ongoing, I had to leave NJA for my wife's treatment in April 2006. Subsequently, the Chief Justice of India prevailed on Dr. Mohan Gopal to take up the position of Director and he assumed office in July 2006.

On my relinquishing office, a grand farewell was given by my colleagues and staff of NJA in which the Chief Justice of India and several judges of the Supreme Court participated. A citation given on the occasion quoted the Resolution adopted by the Governing Board in the following words:

RESOLUTION OF GOVERNING BOARD, NJA, Bhopal

16th April, 2006

"Padmashree Prof. N.R. Madhava Menon, a renowned academician and law teacher par excellence, who pioneered five year LL.B. programme in our country, joined National Judicial Academy on 30th September, 2003 on a personal request made by the then Hon'ble Chief Justice of India. Under his stewardship, National Judicial Academy organized training programmes on a wide variety of subjects, benefiting nearly 2000 judges. It was due to his untiring efforts, intellectual abilities and missionary zeal that the Academy came to be recognized as one of the best centres in the world for imparting judicial education and training.

During Dr. Menon's tenure, the Academy organized training programmes for judges of the Supreme Court of Ghana and Appellate Court of Sri Lanka and an Intellectual Retreat for the Hon'ble Judges of the Supreme Court of India.

Dr. Menon assisted High Courts in the country in setting up State Judicial Academies and trained their respective Directors. National Judicial Academy owes its present status and reputation primarily to Dr. Menon."

I left Bhopal with a sense of satisfaction that I justified my selection to this prestigious position at NJA. It was a learning experience for a law teacher who dealt with students for five decades and then suddenly called upon to initiate judicial training for the higher judiciary. I cherished the experience and consider it a fitting finale to a long career in education and scholarship.

Chapter V

Awaiting Retirement at 75!

AWAITING RETIREMENT AT 75!

Technically I retired thrice in the last fifteen years of my 50 year long legal education career. I took voluntary retirement from Delhi University after 24 years of service with a pension of Rs. 7331 per month. In 1997, I again retired from the service of the National Law School of India University, Bangalore after 12 years of service, of course, without any pensionary benefits. Finally, I retired from the National Judicial Academy, Bhopal in 2006 at the age of 72 thinking that my innings are finally over and I am going to enjoy a retired life with my wife. We wanted to spend time in spiritual pursuits and voluntary social work. This was not to be as later events revealed.

Establlishment of MILAT for Retirement Activity

Well before my return to Trivandrum, several of my students and well wishers set up a registered society by the name of "Menon Institute of Legal Advocacy Training" (MILAT) with a view to engage my spare time in activities of service to society and to the legal profession. I conveyed my interest in devoting time for public legal education and more particularly for citizenship education for youth. In fact, before my retirement from NJA, I prepared a course for "Education for Responsible Citizenship" and tried out its acceptability in a few programmes I conducted on behalf of the Konrad Adenauer Foundation, Delhi. It was so well received by the social activists and students who attended that the Foundation volunteered to publish it as a Training Manual. The idea was to give to the students of the Higher Secondary Schools some minimum understanding of the Rule of Law, Constitutional Governance, Human Rights, the Legal and Judicial System, Fundamental Duties, Electoral System, Intellectual Property Rights and Responsible Citizenship. My plan was to select about 100 students of the 10th standard class who volunteer from city schools in Trivandrum and conduct week-end classes for thirty consecutive weeks. In 2000, I conducted a teacher training programme with support of NCERT in Trivandrum for over 100 teachers from as many schools in the State to encourage them on the subject and to involve them in the conduct of citizenship and human rights education in their respective schools. It was that experience and the Adenauer Foundation experiment which led me to think that it would be an appropriate activity I could undertake in my retirement.

Another activity of my choosing has been continuing education for lawyers and law teachers. MILAT wanted to offer its services in continuing legal education for young advocates free of charge to all interested bar associations in the country. This is something I could confidently undertake because of my long association with the Bar Council of India-sponsored continuing education workshops for Advocates. MILAT conducted a series of five All India Workshops for over 200 law teachers on teaching of skills and ethics. Preparing so many teachers on clinical legal education has been a gratifying and enriching experience personally as it was an activity I was involved in during the later part of my teaching career. I had edited a book on clinical methods of law teaching and floated a Clinical Law Teachers' Association with headquarters in Salgaocar Law College, Goa.

The brief period between June 2006 and September 2007 which I spent in Trivandrum was mostly devoted to these two activities – citizenship education for youth and continuing education for law teachers and lawyers. The Pathanamthitta District Bar Association was the first to invite me for conducting a criminal advocacy workshop. Three days of residential programme of intensive study for 68 young advocates of the district was organized with the help of a retired Supreme Court judge, two sitting High Court judges and three senior advocates. Two more District Bar Associations in Kerala extended the invitation; but before I could organize them I had to shift to Delhi with yet another assignment from the Government of India. However, MILAT collaborated with the IBA Chair on Continuing Education of the National Law School, Bangalore and held a week long workshop for young advocates in September 2008 on the subject of "Trial Advocacy". I discovered that there was great demand for skills development and professional advancement among young advocates and there was no institution in place to respond to their needs. I felt like quitting my newly acquired Government job in Delhi with the Commission on Centre-State Relations and devoting my time in education itself which is my forte. But destiny takes one to unknown destinations and unexpected assignments even when one claims to be in retirement!

Commissions and Committees at Centre and State Levels

I was first asked by the Union Home Minister to help the Government to draft a National Policy on Criminal Justice. This was a follow up to my involvement as a member in the Committee on Criminal Justice Reforms in 2003. A Committee was constituted under my Chairmanship and I got back into active research and writing. No sooner did I complete the report, the Government of India invited me as a Member of the Commission on Centre-State Relations which was set up under the Common Minimum Programme of the UPA Government. I thought as I did with the earlier committees, I could work from Trivandrum along with my MILAT activities, visiting Delhi for short periods as and when required. This was not to be. It turned out to be a full-time employment with very high salaries and perquisites which I never had in my entire service of fifty years. In addition to a house, car, personal staff, I was granted the status of a Union Minister of State! My wife was not enthused and she refused to shift to Delhi for active life again. I was in a dilemma and consulted friends and relatives. My elder sisters advised me that it is good for health in old age to be actively involved in intellectual work and I should not give it up. Many others wondered why I was talking of another full time government job at the age of 73 and advised against it. I commuted between Delhi and Trivandrum almost for an year without occupying the house in Delhi. It did create its own problems at work as well as at home. Finally, after a great deal of deliberation, my wife, finding my interest at work, agreed to shift to Delhi and assist me in completing the assignment. So we shifted again to Delhi after a break of 25 years since we left the Capital in 1986, postponing the retirement for another couple of years.

While working with the Commission on Centre-State Relations, the Government of India got me involved in few other expert committees. These included the Expert Group headed by Dr. T.R. Mashelkar to examine TRIPS compatibility of the amended Patent Act (2005), appointed by the Ministry of Industry & Commerce, a Committee to advise on the methodology to follow in making Judicial Impact Assessment headed by Justice Jagannadha Rao appointed by the Ministry of Law & Justice, and an Expert Committee to Restructure Higher Education with special focus on UGC, AICTE, BCI, MCI etc. chaired by Prof. Yashpal and appointed by the Ministry of Human Resource Development. While working with these Committees as Member, the Ministry of Minority Affairs approached me to Chair an Expert Group to draft a legal framework to establish an Equal Opportunity Commission for India. I became more busy with different types of work as compared to the pre-retirement period!

More than all these Committees and Commissions at the National level, what enthused me most was an invitation to Chair a Committee on Reforms in Legal Education in Kerala appointed by the State Government. For a long time I have had a sort of guilt feeling that I did not do enough for law and legal education in my own State which gave me most of my education including in Law. Therefore, when the Hon'ble Education Minister, Mr. M.A. Baby called me up to request on the assignment I readily accepted it without much hesitation. The Hon'ble Minister even gave me the freedom on the selection of members to be invited for inclusion in the Committee. The Committee formed in August 2008 started its work in right earnest firstly visiting all the law colleges in the state and interacting with teachers and students of every college, including the college where I studied for LL.B. almost 55 years ago, the Government Law College, Trivandrum. I personally felt sad that despite all the progress legal education made elsewhere in India, the system followed in most colleges in Kerala followed the same pattern adopted half a century ago. I admired the initiative of the Communist Government of the State for having decided to end this neglect and give legal education its due. I started devoting considerable time to reflect on the steps to be followed for reforming the quality of legal education and persuaded the teachers and students to start dreaming big and be prepared to welcome the changes now under way. There was excitement in a large section of students and some subdued enthusiasm in a section of teachers. The atmosphere was cynical and most people conveyed their impression that nothing would change in Kerala as power-brokers and political parties would not allow things to happen which even remotely may affect their vested interests. I did not believe it as I found the Education Minister, an influential member of the Government and party is very much committed to reforms. He told me that he would start implementing the recommendations within two months of submission of the Report. The Committee therefore decided to submit the report before the commencement of the new academic year and worked overtime to complete it. The Report was submitted in July, 2009. Unlike other Committees, I was even prepared to take a role in its implementation if the Government so desired. My wife was cautioning me against taking another plunge, this time a little controversial in the home State of Kerala and that too at the age of 75!

Life moves on and new expectations and resolutions replace the old. Health is deteriorating and body is asking to slow down activities. Mind, on the other hand, seems to say that lot many things need to be done and can be done before one bids good bye to this wonderful, beautiful world. I am reminded of what Robert Frost had written many years ago:

> The woods are lovely, dark and deep
> But I have promises to keep
> And miles to go before I sleep
> And miles to go before I sleep

Chapter VI

Recollections and Remembrances from Friends & Well-wishers

A TRIBUTE TO DR. MENON

I regard, with reverence and pride, Dr. N.R. Madhava Menon as among the rarest of the rare who have made Indian Legal Education qualitatively attain a progressive transformation, beyond the dream of the Victorian vintage architects of legal education which was feudal, colonial and lacking in that creativity and native genius which is a *sine qua non* of truly sublime legal education. Never in the field of Indian legal education was so much owed by so many to so few as tens of thousands of students of law owe to celebrated doyen Dr. Madhava Menon and a few like him. Dr. Madhava Menon is a marvel in the transformation process of Indian legal education. He has made himself immortal by his original contribution in the field of Law and Justice. The great institutions of legal education in Bangalore and Calcutta are historic creations and the credit goes to Dr. Menon.

I have known Dr. Madhava Menon for long, appreciated his capacity as a teacher in the Delhi University, with a deep grasp of jurisprudence, especially criminal law. He is not a traditional professor but an original scholar introducing new ideas and subjects with a facility and felicity that makes his thoughts so refreshing. I have seen him at work in the Delhi University but he was at his best in the Bangalore Law School University which was virtually his creation. Victimology, as a branch of criminal justice, was made part of the study in the Law University by his effort. Other instances of originality can be cited, like persuading final year students to go into villages and make practical studies of rural conditions from the angle of legal rights. This is a remarkable dimension to legal education in a competitive spirit. Providence fashions a genius, it has been well said, and breaks its mould so that another imitator hardly emerges. That is why Dr. Menon has no parallel. For him, the integrality of law and justice is a democratic necessity, and the first chapter of the book is an inspiration in itself. He is not flamboyant, as some other pedagogic jurists are. His sobriety in presentation as a teacher and writer of law has been impressive without being flashy.

The extraordinary originality with which he innovated the idea of a college of judicial education and made it remarkable reality of it as a going concern of training and upgradation for the benefit of the higher judiciary is commendable. This is an institutional wonder of which Menon is the founder, although officially former Chief Justices had triggered this thought and sought to install an institution at Bhopal. The perspective of judicial education takes shape only when a plan is prepared, a project is implemented and a great academic thought gains pragmatic locomotion. We have such a college now in Bhopal and this is no mean achievement of Menon. Bhopal is a lasting tribute to him as one who founded such a college which has done so much to raise the standard or equipment of the higher judiciary in India.

I must conclude because brevity is a necessity of age and illness. Nevertheless, a tribute to Dr. Menon is a moral obligation which I discharge with delight. Every reader of the book will be richer as he reaches the last page. My eye sight is poor but my mind sight is lost in deep appreciation of the magnificent biography. I congratulate Dr. S. Surya Prakash for his devotion in immortalizing the life of a great son of India. I salute you, Dr. Menon.

November 19, 2008 V.R. KRISHNA IYER

DR. N.R. MADHAVA MENON: A SPECIAL NAME

Dr. N.R. Madhava Menon is a special name to be remembered wherever and whenever legal education in India is discussed. Though, I could get only a few opportunities to associate with him, they were good enough to enable me to form the opinion that he is a legal personage with a difference. I firmly believe that he turned the tide of legal education in such a manner that law, as a subject of studies, became attractive, more attractive than other conventional subjects.

When I joined law college for degree course in late nineteen fifties, quite a number of persons known to me frowned at my choice because law education was then considered to be a pursuit of the lazy and happy go lucky students. That trend has now been reversed. If I am asked to focus on one person responsible for this revolution, I would unhesitatingly point to Dr. N.R. Madhava Menon.

As Chairman of the Statutory Review Committee of National Law School University of Bangalore, I had occasion to hear from different segments of persons associated with that institution how it grew up and blossomed. The other members of the committee were Dr. Virendra Kumar, Chairman of Department of Laws, Punjab University and Dr. M.P. Singh, Vice Chancellor of West Bengal National University of Juridical Science, Kolkota. We heard from almost all those who interacted with us how splendidly Dr. N.R. Madhava Menon charioted the Law School during its infantile years and how he converted it into the most prestigious law teaching institution in India, the fame of which had transcended beyond the boundaries of the nation.

When Supreme Court of India was in search of the appropriate person to be the Director of National Judicial Academy (Bhopal) Dr. N.R. Madhava Menon became the unanimous choice of all the judges. I learnt that it was an uphill task for the then Chief Justice of India to persuade him to accept the assignment. Dr. Menon felt that training judges in India is different from training budding legal talents. Finally he yielded and took up the administration of the academy which was then in the nascent stage studded with several problems. I have no hesitation to acknowledge the fact that Dr. N.R. Madhava Menon made the institution to reach the stage of national recognition.

The simple living and the informal way of doing things of Dr. Menon impressed me a lot. When the golden jubilee of his career as law teacher is being celebrated, I wish to sum up like this:

> "Law education in India owes much to Dr. N.R. Madhava Menon".

June 15, 2009.

JUSTICE K.T. THOMAS
Former Judge, Supreme Court of India

A FITTING TRIBUTE

I am very glad to know about the biography of Prof. N.R. Madhava Menon under the title TURNING POINT'. It is a fitting tribute to one of our greatest academicians in law who has given a new direction to legal education in India. As founder Vice Chancellor of the National Law School of India University, Bangalore, his effort has set in motion revolutionary changes in the improvement and importance of legal education and has given rise to a number of National Law Universities in several parts of this country. Today, our students are grabbing several international awards as well as employment in leading law firms abroad and within our own country. Prof. Menon has also contributed to vast improvement in the quality of teaching.

He has also distinguished himself as the first Director of the National Judicial Academy, Bhopal for training Judges in the subordinate judiciary and for starting programmes in continuing the legal/judicial education for judges at all levels.

I have been associated with him both at the National Law School, Banglore as well as at the National Judicial Academy at Bhopal. In Delhi, we worked together in the Sub-Committee of the National Knowledge Commission on Legal Education, and also in the Committee appointed by the Government, on the suggestion of the Supreme Court, for proposing a scheme for Judicial Impact Assessment. We have been together in several conferences also. I was always impressed by his originality in matters concerning legal education, judicial reforms, continuing legal/judicial education, administrative frame work of Judiciary and for institutions teaching law. I wish all success in publishing the biography of one of the great sons of India.

June 14, 2009.

JUSTICE M. JAGANNADHA RAO
Formerly, Judge Supreme Court of India,
Formerly, Chairman, Law Commission of India

ONCE A TEACHER ALWAYS A TEACHER

I was first introduced to Prof. N.R. Madhava Menon, when he was Director of National Law School of Juridical Sciences, Calcutta and I was Chief Justice of High Court of Gujarat.

On 26th January, 2001, earthquake shook Gujarat rendering thousands dead, injured, roofless and children orphan.

In a PIL, our bench passed an order containing several directions to the Government that relief material and donations for help coming from India and abroad should reach all victims really in distress and need. To oversee the relief operations, our Bench directed that services of District Judges, who were *ex-offico* Chairpersons of Legal Services Authority, be utilized in the capacity of Ombudsmen In issuing such directions in PIL, we invoked the Doctrine of Public Trust and insisted the State to play its role as a Public Trustee for management and distribution of relief materials and cash received as donations from all over the world for the earthquakes victims.

Prof. Menon, a vigilant law-man as he is, took prompt cognizance of the intervention made by the High Court. He not-only congratulated me and the High Court for quick and timely judicial intervention in an emergent situation but to support the court order sent a team of students headed by teachers from his Law Institution to undertake a field study of the conditions of the quake affected people and suggest legal remedies.

My contact with Prof. Menon was renewed at Bhopal during my periodic visits to the National Judicial Academy for training programmes for Judges. We chaired few Panels together. I was deeply impressed not-only by his width and depth of knowledge in law, but his sensitivity and passion for the plight of marginal and deprived sections of Indian People, who endlessly wait for justice in our present slow moving judicial system.

I have heard and read with interest his speeches and writings in which he passionately pleads and appeals for improving our Justice-Delivery-System for realisation of recognized constitutional rights by vast deprived sections of our Indian Society.

Our Constitution in Article 124(3)(c) provides for appointment of distinguished jurists as Judges of Supreme Court.

A person of legal caliber and character as Prof. Menon amply fits in the description of word "Jurist" as envisaged in our Constitution.

On completion of 75 years of his age, I heartily congratulate him and earnestly wish and hope that he would continue to guide and inspire our young generation.

Let me remind him: "***Once a teacher always a teacher***". Teaching qualities improve with advancing age.

Bhopal
May 29, 2009.

JUSTICE D.M. DHARMADHIKARI
Former Judge, Supreme Court of India
Former Chief Justice High Court of Gujarat
Chairperson, M.P. Human Rights Commission

MY IMPRESSIONS OF PROF. N.R. MADHAVA MENON

I was first introduced to Professor N.R. Madhava Menon in 1980's when Prof. Menon was a teacher in the Law Faculty of Delhi University and I was an Advocate practicing in the Orissa High Court. I had been to New Delhi in connection with a case before the Supreme Court and when I was working on my brief with my senor Shri Ranjeet Mohanty, who was then the Chairman of the Bar Council of India, Prof. Menon walked into the office of the Chairman, Bar Council of India for discussions on the proposed National Law School of India University at Bangalore. The National Law School of India University was established in Bangalore and Prof. Menon became its first Director (Vice-Chancellor) and within a short time, Prof. Menon was able to turn the National Law School of India University to an institution of excellence in the study of Law.

In 1996, when I was a Judge of the Gauhati High Court, I again met Prof. Menon during my visit to National Law School of India University, Bangalore. He took me around the University and showed me the different facilities provided for the law students. I was impressed by the immense contribution made by Prof. Menon to the teaching of law in India. Prior to the establishment of the National Law School of India University, Bangalore, teaching of law in various Law Colleges was casual and students would start studying their subjects only a few days before the LL.B. examinations. But in the National Law School of India University, there was rigorous teaching of social sciences and law for the students studying the five years LL.B. course. The product of the National Law School of India University was in great demand by the corporate houses and students passing out from the National Law School of India University were offered huge salary packages and the rush for admission to the National Law School of University, Bangalore, started. Consequently, National Law University with five years LL.B.

course was planned in other states like Andhra Pradesh, Chattisgarh, Delhi, Gujarat, Madhya Pradesh, Rajasthan and West Bengal etc.

In 2002, I was transferred from the Gauhati High Court to the Orissa High Court and in 2003, I was the Judge in-charge of the Judicial Officers' Training in Orissa. Around the same time, Prof. Menon became the Director of the National Judicial Academy, Bhopal. As soon as the Orissa Judicial Academy at Cuttack was ready for inauguration, we invited Prof. Menon to be the Guest of Honour to the inaugural function at which Shri Justice Arijit Pasayat, then a judge of the Supreme Court, was the Chief Guest. At the inaugural function Prof. Menon addressed the gathering on judicial training and I was impressed by the information that he had on judicial training in US and other countries. In 2003, there were meetings of the High Court Judges in-charge of judicial training and the Directors of the Judicial Officers Training Institutes of different States at the National Judicial Academy at Bhopal. Shri Justice Jagannath Rao, former Judge of the Supreme Court and Shri Justice Malimath, former Chief Justice of the High Court of Karnataka and Prof. Mohan Gopal who is presently the Director of the National Judicial Academy at Bhopal, were also present in the meetings. We had number of sessions on the curriculum for the foundation training of the judicial officers recruited as Civil Judge Class II. Prof. Menon impressed upon all of us that training of judicial officers was not to be like law class teaching and instead should focus on inculcating in the judicial officers appropriate skills and qualities to become a good judge. During 2003-2006, I visited the National Judicial Academy at Bhopal several times and I was impressed by the novel methods he adopted for training of judicial officers of our country.

In 2005, I assumed charge as the Chief Justice of Chattisgarh High Court and was the *ex-officio* Chancellor of the Hidayatullah National Law University at Raipur. There was then no Vice-Chancellor in the Hidayatullah National Law University and search committee comprising Shri Justice Malimath as Chairman and Prof. Menon and Shri Jagannath Patnaik (the then Chairman of the Bar Council of India) as members met at Raipur and submitted a panel of three names for appointment of the Vice-Chancellor and out of this panel, Dr. M.K. Srivastava was appointed as the Vice-Chancellor of the Hidayatullah National Law University, Raipur. In October 2005, I was transferred to the Madhya Pradesh High Court as the Chief Justice of the Madhya Pradesh High Court and was the Chairman General Council of the National Law Institute University, Bhopal. Within a month or two of my assuming charge as the Chief Justice of the Madhya Pradesh High Court, the then Vice-Chancellor of the national Law Institute

University, Bhopal, resigned to become the Secretary of the University Grants Commission. A search Committee of which Prof. Menon was a member, submitted a panel of three names and the Chief Justice of India, who was Visitor of the University, selected Prof. Balraj Chauhan as the director of the National Law Institute University, Bhopal. As member of two search committees, Prof. Menon had focused in selecting persons with knowledge of law and the ability to administer as Vice-Chancellor and Director of the two law universities.

After Prof. Menon left the National Judicial Academy Bhopal, he wrote a number of articles in the news papers on legal education, the role of Bar Councils and the legal system of our country and some reviews on different books on our judicial and legal system. His analysis on the different subjects in these articles and his book reviews reveal his insight and depth into the judicial and legal system of our country and provide food for thought for anyone who is interested in bringing about legal and judicial reforms in India.

I am happy to learn that Dr. S. Surya Prakash is preparing a Biography on Prof. N. R. Madhava Menon titled "Turning Point". The contributions of Prof. Menon to legal education, judicial training, selection of teachers and Vice-Chancellor/director in Law Universities and in shaping up the best minds in law and judiciary of this country must be acknowledged.

June 20, 2009. A.K. PATNAIK

Chief Justice of Madhya Pradesh

PROF. N.R. MADHAVA MENON – A PRECIOUS ASSET OF THE NATION

Prof. N.R. Madhava Menon is an outstanding jurist and shining star in the world of law. He left indelible imprints on every field he has touched whether as law teacher, reformer of legal education, a builder of excellent institutions for legal education, as an author, as a critic, as an orator, as a thinker and as a researcher. He has a very keen and analytical mind. He is a great thinker. He is voracious reader and prolific writer. The wide and impressive range of his contributions has left an impression that he can provide answers to every type of problem. That is why he is invited to contribute as a member of various committees. His contribution as a member of the Committee on Reforms of Criminal Justice Systems, of which I was Chairman is outstanding. He has made valuable contribution as a Member of the Committee on drafting a National Policy on criminal justice and as a member on drafting the National Police Act. He is presently engaged as a member of National Commission on Inter-State Relations. He has made tremendous contribution in solving wide range of problems facing the country. His versatility, humility and readiness to serve the country are his most notable qualities. Like him is not easy to find. Prof. Madhava Menon is a precious asset and pride of our nation.

Bangalore
June 1, 2009.

DR. JUSTICE V.S. MALIMATH
Chairman
Law Commission of Karnataka

LEGAL SCHOLAR NON-PAREIL

Can anyone who is exposed to Law and Law Teaching "crib, crab and confine" Dr. Menon into a capsule. To describe him as multi-faceted and multi-dimensional is to encase him in a cocoon. To say that he is a Law Teacher who conquered new frontiers does not do full justice to his immense and immeasurable contribution to the field of Law. To refer to him as a trail-blazer and trend setter and explorer on a voyage of discovery of the expanding horizons of law making and law teaching would not render full justice to his unique contribution to the growth of law and law teaching. He is something more and to attempt a profile of this innovative and creative Law Teacher is beyond anybody's competence. Dr. Menon is a self-made man and from the Aligarh University, Delhi University and the Bar Council of India Trust to grow to be the founder Director of the National Law School, Bangalore was a journey of toil and triumph. If the Bar Council of India has something to boast about, it is the establishment of National Law School of India University, Bangalore and the idea caught on and it is replicated in several States and today we have such institutions of excellence in a dozen States and many such institutions in other States are in the pipeline. We do not have an IVY LEAGUE. We speak of Havard, Yale, Stanford Universities with awe as Centres of Excellence in the field of Legal Education. Dr. Menon by his untiring efforts, vision and foresight built up a citadel of legal education which vies with the prestigious American Law institutions mentioned above.

In the city of gardens, Bangalore, now known as "Benguluru", on the green fields of Nagarbhavi, Dr. Menon the master craftsman and architect built up a great center of learning brick by brick. A founder of any great institution requires vision and should have the consciousness that every stone that is placed will be a milestone for the future and it is not brick and mortar or cement that alone are required to build a massive structure but it is the qualities of the head and the heart of the founder, his creativity that enables to build an institution that has everlasting values in the ever – changing scenario of law. Dr. Menon gave the best years of his life to the building up of this great Law School in Bangalore. A tireless crusader for the pursuit of excellence, he moved to attain the objective of establishing the National Law School, Bangalore, moved on to Calcutta to build the National University of Juridical Sciences and from there he turned his attention to the National Judicial Academy, Bhopal which is an institution meant for training the Judiciary and for imparting to them knowledge of the new vistas of the explosive expansion of Law in all its myriad dimensions. Not only District Judges, Judges of the High Court and even Judges of the Supreme Court find it a rewarding and refreshing experience to spend some time in the National Judicial Academy. That the Judges of the Highest Court of the land conferred the honour of making him the first Director of the National Judicial Academy was the crowning glory of this many-splendoured achiever.

After you scale mount Everest what other height can you attain? Dr. Menon's commitment is to bring about a sea-change in Legal Education. This restless soul toiled ceaselessly to improve the standard of legal education. Dr. Menon is an uncompromising individual and has the courage of his conviction and he calls a spade a spade and some times more than a spade. His trenchant criticism of the proliferation of substandard Law Schools invited the wrath of some of the members of Bar Council of India. His criticism of the role of the Bar was also not appreciated by many members of the profession but in the end Dr. Menon's real intentions were understood and appreciated by many in the Bar and the Bar Council. His anxiety and concern for improvement of legal education and promotion of higher standards of professional conduct were appreciated and in that sense his well meaning criticism was understood and his desire for improving the tone and tenor of legal education and Advocacy was very well received. His mission is a continuing odyssey. Having attained the pinnacle of Directorship of National Judicial Academy he could have rested on his oars and retreat into a self imposed sun-set. The unquenchable thirst for promoting and sharing knowledge in law urged him to start MILAT a programme for training young Lawyers.

Dr. Menon's contribution did not stop with improvement of legal education and Government of India whenever it thought of Law always invited Dr. Menon to assist them. As a member of the Law Commission of India, as a Member of Justice Mallimath Committee appointed by the Government of India for suggesting reforms in the Criminal Justice System, he made enormous contribution to suggest reforms of far reaching nature. As a member of the Police Act Drafting

Committee and Chairman of the Committee to Draft a National Policy on Criminal Justice he served the Government. No wonder when the Government of India appointed Dr. Sam Pitroda to head the Knowledge Commission Dr. Menon was called upon to assist the Knowledge Commission for devising a blue print for legal education reform taking into account the emerging trends. When the Government of India thought of a fresh look into the Centre-State relation under the Constitution of India, Dr. Menon was made its Member. When the Government thought of setting up an Equal Opportunity Commission, Dr. Menon was asked to Chair the Expert Group. Again when Yashpal Committee was appointed to suggest reforms in higher education, Dr. Menon was called upon to be its member. The Government of Kerala invited him to Chair a Committee on reforming legal education in the State.

I had the good fortune of knowing him personally for more than 20 years and had occasion to work with him when he was a member of the Legal Education Committee of the Bar Council of India and also a member of Justice Mallimath Committee. In any meeting or group discussion you would always find him making copious notes in his wonderful handwriting and before the meeting concluded invariably he would come up with his concrete views or recommendations. For him work is worship and he never wasted a minute in his zeal for change. In the Bar Council when members had occasions to feel uncomfortable when he was unsparing in his criticism of some of the unedifying facets of the profession, his transparent sincerity carried the day and Bar appreciated his stand ultimately. The many articles that he wrote and published in Law Journals in India and abroad and news papers are eloquent testimony of a teacher's commitment to share his knowledge with others.

In paying my tribute to him, my proximity to him has not blurred my vision. The assessment of Dr. Menon in these few lines is objective and is the result of both shared experiences and also an admirer's observation from a distance. When law and legal profession raise a toast for him, a Padma Award means nothing for him. Dr. Menon is not merely an institution builder he is himself an institution and all I can say is **"here is a great teacher par excellence, when comes such another"**.

July 30, 2009.

D.V. SUBBA RAO
Former Chairman, Bar Council of India

JUST ONE PERSON
DR. N.R. MADHAVA MENON

I have had occasion to interact with Dr. Madhava Menon over the last few decades and have always admired his total dedication to the cause of legal education in India and abroad.

When the National Law School of India University, Banglore was set up in 1987, legal education in India was in doldrums, and hundreds of law schools were set up all over India without proper infrastructure and teaching staff. This sadly reflected on the quality of lawyers turned out by these institutions and services rendered by the legal profession to the clientele. It was then that Dr. Madhava Menon persuaded the Bar Council of India and the Government of Karnataka to co-operate in passing legislation for setting up the NLSIU. The methodology used for teaching the various legal subjects was in keeping the techniques used in the best universities abroad. The method of selection of students itself was wholly devoid of nepotism and influence, which I should say was unique for our country. The students who graduated could compete with the best among lawyers in any part of the world. The face of legal education in India changed dramatically.

The success of NLSIU can be gauged from the fact that every State in the country is vying with each other in setting up national law universities on the same lines of NLSIU. The law graduates turned out by these institutions were picked up through campus placements by law firms, foreign and Indian, and by multinational corporations.

All changes can be attributed to just one person, namely, Dr. N.R. Madhava Menon. I remember a suggestion he made to me that I should sponsor a national law university in Kerala. We together met the then Chief Minister who fully supported the scheme. We even met the famous architect, Laurie Baker, who was based in Trivandrum, as we believed that the project would materialize. Dr. Madhava Menon was prepared to give up all other assignments to establish the national law university in Kerala. Unfortunately, for various reasons, the project failed though.

I remember that one of his proposals was for SAARC Law, which is an association of lawyers and judges of SAARC countries, to either sponsor law universities on the lines of NLSIU in each one of the SAARC countries or have campuses which would turn out law graduates, who would be of the same caliber as those coming out of the National Law Universities in India.

Unfortunately, SAARC Law was unable to implement his vision in this regard.

I would have no doubt in my mind that Dr. N.R. Madhava Menon is the person solely responsible for catapulating law teaching in India to international standards, to compete with best universities abroad.

June 7, 2009.

K.K. VENUGOPAL
Senior Advocate
Supreme Court of India,

THE GREATEST LAW TEACHER

My heartiest congratulations to Dr. Madhava Menon on his completing 50 years as a Teacher. I have been privileged to know him for more than twenty-five of those fifty years. He is in my opinion one of the greatest law teachers we have had in India. Will Durant has defined "Education as the technique of transmitting civilization". Dr. Madhava Menon is the living embodiment of that noble definition.

FALI S. NARIMAN
President
The Bar Association of India

A TRIBUTE TO PROFESSOR MADHAVA MENON *from the* COMMONWEALTH LEGAL EDUCATION ASSOCIATION

I first met Professor Menon in February 1995 when he was still Dean of the National Law School of India University in Bangalore, and I was invited to conduct part of a workshop for paralegals at the Law School. The workshop was typical of Professor Menon's initiatives to reach out to communities beyond the traditional university ivory tower and had attracted paralegals from a wide variety of community based organisations.

I took over the Presidency of the Commonwealth Legal Education Association (CLEA) from Professor Menon in 1997, and although it is over ten years since he relinquished his Presidency Professor Menon's influence is still strongly felt. In his 1994 inaugural address Professor Menon had suggested that CLEA needed: (a) to make legal education socially relevant and professionally useful; (b) to encourage law schools to prepare themselves for the demands of the profession in the context of the information revolution and other global challenges; (c) to support continuing legal education and distance learning programmes; and (d) encourage law schools to critically look at their law curricula and teaching methods.

The plan of action suggested by Professor Menon continues to guide the activities of CLEA. The result is that today CLEA focuses on: (a) the training of law teachers; (b) the development of and support for research; (c) improving law library facilities; (d) developing the use of electronically produced data; (e) curriculum development; (f) professional training; (g) strengthening links between Commonwealth law schools; and (h) strengthening clinical legal education and law clinics in the Commonwealth.

I had the pleasure of hosting Professor Menon in South Africa when I was President of the Society of Law Teachers of South Africa and invited him to be the guest speaker at our biannual conference in 1997. Since then I have shared international and local conference platforms with him on several occasions in countries such as India, Malaysia and China. For me it is always a great privilege and a pleasure to hear him speak because his words and thoughts are not only very original but also highly inspirational. It matters not whether his audience is composed of judges, academics, law students, paralegals or bare foot social activists Professor Menon always promotes his message about the importance of the law and lawyers in securing social justice for ordinary people, particularly the poor and marginalised.

Professor Menon has 'retired' on several occasions only to be recalled to establish new and exciting initiatives in Indian legal education – many of which were originally conceived by him.

It is difficult to believe that Professor Menon will be celebrating his 75th birthday this year. He has the intellectual agility and energy of a person twenty years younger. Maybe it has something to do with Mrs. Menon and her wonderfully healthy cooking that accompanies him wherever he goes!

It gives me great pleasure on behalf of CLEA and my colleagues throughout the Commonwealth to wish Professor Menon a happy 75th birthday and to join with him in celebrating his 50th year of teaching. Long may he enjoy many more 'retirements'!

June 16, 2009.

PROFESSOR DAVID MCQUOID-MASON
President, Commonwealth Legal Education Association;
Co-Vice-Chair International Bar Association Academic
and Professional Development Committee and
Acting Director Centre for Socio-Legal Studies,
University of KwaZulu-Natal, Durban, South Africa

REMINISCENCES OF WORKING WITH DR. N.R. MADHAVA MENON

I first met Dr. Menon in 1985 when he was Head of the Faculty at the Campus Law Center at Delhi University and I was about to apply for a Fulbright grant to teach in India. He was immediately positive about the idea and paved the way for me to serve as a Fulbright Senior Lecturer and Visiting Professor of Law at Delhi University during the academic year 1986-87. Since then, we have worked together on many occasions. I visited the National Law School of India University a number of times during his tenure as Founding Director (and also later at the National University of Juridical Science), we chaired the inaugural meeting of the Global Alliance for Justice Education (GAJE), and we have taught together at various clinical teacher training workshops sponsored by the Menon Institute of Legal Advocacy and Training (MILAT).

Delhi University

My project during my Fulbright year at Delhi University focused on legal aid and clinical legal education, fields in which Dr. Menon was already a leading figure in India. I was struck immediately by his energy and creativity, together with his unique collegial approach to faculty governance. His strong personal commitment to legal education reform was well known, including his vision of how clinical programs could enhance both professional skills training and law students' awareness of their public professional responsibility. Although there were already a number of legal aid clinics at the Campus Law Center, he asked me to explore and suggest ways that clinical legal education might be advanced not just at Delhi University but throughout India. Most importantly, he encouraged me to engage as many of his colleagues as I could in the process so that they would be informed when proposals for new courses or projects would come before the faculty. Then, when we discussed our ideas for reform he would invite groups of colleagues to join us. We would all sit around a large table placed in front of his desk, which to me was a remarkable physical symbol of the openness and transparency with which he carried out his duties as Head of the Faculty. Dr. Menon and I also began working on a manuscript of what would later become a handbook on clinical legal education in India. This same approach of informing others about—and engaging them in—clinical legal education marked his efforts to expand the clinical movement in India. Thus, later in the year he encouraged me to talk about legal aid and clinical legal education to law faculty, lawyers, and judges around the country and facilitated a lecture tour that took me to campuses and cities from Kolkata to Mumbai to Chennai.

National Law School of India University

I had the opportunity to visit with Dr. Menon when the National Law School of India University was still on the drawing boards in a suite of offices at Bangalore University, and many times since then at the law school campus. Having already decided to include clinical legal education in the model curriculum he was developing for the law school, Dr. Menon took special care to make sure that the clinical program contributed most effectively to his agenda of legal education reform. One way he did that was to obtain a grant for faculty enrichment from the Ford Foundation. One of the first of his colleagues to use the grant was Professor V. Nagaraj, who came to Vanderbilt University Law School for a semester to learn about and work in our clinical program. When Professor Nagaraj returned to Bangalore to assume responsibility for the law school's clinical program, Dr. Menon asked him to organize an extensive workshop on clinical teaching that brought together clinical teachers from India, Australia, the US, and the UK. The workshop covered all aspects of clinical legal education, from course content to teaching methods. Material prepared for that workshop was then included in the handbook manuscript begun years earlier at Delhi University, which was published by the Eastern Book Co. in 1998.

Global Alliance for Justice Education (GAJE)

Dr. Menon played two key roles in the creation of the Global Alliance for Justice Education (GAJE). In 1996, he presented the keynote address entitled *In Defense of Socially Relevant Legal Education* at the 19th Annual Clinical Education Conference of the Association of American Law Schools in Miami. Two meetings were held during that conference, attended by Dr. Menon, myself, and other conference delegates from the US and a number of other countries, during which the idea of forming GAJE was first discussed. Three years later, Dr. Menon and I co-chaired the inaugural meeting of that organization in Dr. Menon's home town. Not only did that conference establish GAJE as an international organization, but it also set the tone of the organization and its four subsequent global conferences held in South Africa, Poland, Argentina, and the Philippines. Noteworthy aspects of the inaugural conference program initiated by Dr. Menon were an inspiring opening speech by Justice V.R. Krishna Iyer, home hospitality for foreign delegates hosted by the families of students from local law schools, and a visit to a *lok adalat* where delegates could observe law students participating as part of their clinical program.

Menon Institute of Legal Advocacy and Training (MILAT)

Dr. Menon's commitment to clinical legal education has been institutionalized in the Menon Institute of Legal Advocacy and Training (MILAT). Through MILAT, Dr. Menon has organized and run a series of workshops in an effort to create a cadre of well-trained clinical law teachers in India. He has invited a few clinical teachers from outside India (including me) to join him and other Indian clinical teachers as workshop faculty, but it is his presence at these workshops and his vision for clinical education in India that inspires the young professors who attend. Always looking to the future, he is in the process of putting together a new book on clinical education and clinical teaching methods that will help guide the future of the Indian clinical legal education movement. And most remarkably, he carries on his activities at MILAT despite his many other responsibilities since his "retirement" (including, most recently, membership on the Commission on Centre-State Relations).

His perseverance and commitment to the cause of legal education has made him a remarkable person in the history of legal education in India. His biography is aptly titled "Turning Point" and is a right tribute to Prof. Menon who has changed the course of legal education in India.

FRANK S. BLOCH
Professor of Law & Director, Social Justice Program
Vanderbilt University Law School (USA)

June 29, 2009.

THE MENON PHENO'MENON'

What a piece of work is man ! This is Shakespeare in Hamlet.

What a piece of work is Madhava Menon ! This is the refrain of Legal fraternity in contemporary India. How noble in commitment and how marvellous as a builder of institutions is Prof. N.R. Madhava Menon.

If the Legal education scenario presents the bright manifestation of the Benchmarks of excellence, that is the genre of National Legal Schools today, it is because of the foresight of this legal luminary and farsighted wisdom of this extra ordinary crusader of perfection in whatever he undertakes.

1987 marks a beginning of a glorious era in the history of legal education in India when the National Law school was established at Bangalore. Starting it as an experiment in Legal education where innovation is given the highest priority, Prof. Madhava Menon as its founder Director laid the strong foundations with his unswerving commitment, dedication and zeal and so strong has been the foundation that " NLS today has become a victim of its own success". Prof. Menon has in his inimitable manner took a pledge-"Enough has been heard of the cliché that India has a tradition of producing brilliant and outstanding lawyers in spite of its Law Colleges and time has come for us to prove that quality law graduates can be produced by the Law Schools". With the Bar Council of India 's noble decision to start the Five Year course and to start a School for providing Quality Legal Education, Prof. Menon relentlessly strived for translating the BCI's dream into a reality. He was the Director for ten years a decade which has come to be known as a DECADE OF ACHIEVEMENT in Legal Education. If today, one finds the spectre of Law Schools imparting excellent legal education throughout the length and breadth of the country, it is because of the trend setting and epoch making phenomenon of the NLS, Bangalore. First is always the First. This First is the First today because of the missionary zeal with which Prof. Menon developed the work culture in the NLS. We are grateful to him.

If the NLS has become synonymous with excellence, it is because Prof. Menon has been synonymous with NLS in its formative years. First Banglore, then Calcutta and then Bhopal (where the National Judicial Academy is established)—Prof. Menon has been the founder Director in all these places and all of them are today centres of excellence.

Can there be a greater tribute to this no-nonsense navigator than the adored success of these institutions which are acclaimed all over as the best of their kind. In short, Prof. Madhava Menon is a phenomenon.

The only question is : Whence comes the next.

June 30, 2009.

PROF. R. VENKATA RAO
Vice-Chancellor, NLSIU, Bangalore.

PROF. N.R. MADHVA MENON "AS I KNOW HIM"

Sometimes in life, it becomes difficult to pen down your thoughts when you are asked to write about a person whom you not only respect, love, adore but also relate yourself with emotionally and try to follow his footprints so that you may get accolade, appreciation and patting on your back. I had the similar experience when my learned colleague and younger brother Prof. S. Surya Prakash of National Law Institute University, Bhopal asked me to pen down my memories with Prof. N.R. Madhva Menon. I understand fully well that it will not be an easy task for a person like me who has a limited vocabulary, power of expression and the inability to reflect feelings of heart and soul into appropriate words. However, I consider it my proud privilege and feel honoured to share my thoughts about a person who has influenced and transformed the lives of many, including me.

Going down the memory lane I recall when, for the first time, I came across the name of Prof. N.R. Madhva Menon. It was in 1977 when I was pursuing LL.M course with specialization in Criminal Law and Criminology, my teacher Dr. Pramod Kumar (whom I consider as a *guru* as he taught me the ABC of Criminal Law so that I may understand the principles of Criminal Justice Administration) asked me to read the article of Prof. Menon published in the Lucknow Law Journal in 1967-68 which was a seminar special issue on teaching and research in Criminal Law and Criminology. Prof. Menon's article was on "Scientific Investigation of Crime and the Judicial Process in India". I am quoting here a few lines from his article.

> "Crime detection is becoming more and more a specialized, complicated, and often times an expensive job for which the investigation officer and the prosecuting agencies shall have to be trained and equipped."

In the second part he writes, "They are: Physical and Medical examination of the accused; comparison of fingerprints, footprints, hand-writing and photographs; forensic ballistics; tape-recording, wire-tapping and other means of electronic surveillance and eavesdropping; deception test with the help of lie-detector and the administration of truth serum etc. The above list is not exhaustive but only illustrative." The lines written by Prof. Menon in 1967 are still relevant in the administration of Criminal Justice in India and serve as beacon light as far as the matter of scientific investigation of crime is concerned.

In 1978, after completing LL.M., I joined Lucknow University as a Lecturer in Law leaving other options such as administrative jobs, banks etc. That was the time when Legal Education was not taken in the highest esteem and there were only few students who were interested in serious discussions and studies. I remember that I used Prof. Menon's articles for discussions especially with LL.M. students. During the 1980s discussions on truth serum, lie detector evidence used to create sharp discussions in the class. One day when I was sitting in the Teachers' room of the Law Faculty, suddenly the name of Prof. Menon echoed in the corridors because Prof. R.C. Vyas, Prof. G.S. Pandey and other teachers who attended the All India Law Teachers Conference at Bareilly were discussing the proposal made by Prof. Menon to stretch the LL.B. programme from three years to five years. Teachers were divided on the issue and most of them were apprehensive about its success. Similar voices and reactions were raised by very senior Professors from all over the country. Up to that period, I never had the opportunity to meet Prof. Menon personally, yet I knew him through Prof. L.N. Tandon, Prof. G.S. Sharma, Prof. Pramod Kumar and friends from Delhi University. I remember for the first time I met Prof. Menon at Delhi University where I had gone to consult the Library and I found him there and for a few minutes I had a brief discussion with him; of course it was not of a very serious nature.

Prof. Menon was the Secretary of Bar Council of India Trust also and I guessed from my discussions with other Faculty Members of Delhi University that he still was for integrated five year B.A. LL.B. programme. Today Prof. Menon is known as an institution builder, the architect of five year integrated B.A. LL.B programme because as a teacher, as a person and as a jurist whatever he preached, he practised that too.

In 1990, when for the first time I got the opportunity to be with Prof. Menon for about a month at NLSIU, Bangalore as a Vice-Chancellor of the University, I found him to be a hard task master working more than 12 hours a day in the office; as a teacher ready to share his knowledge with juniors like me, interacting with us and at that time forcing us to think beyond classroom teaching, adopting new pedagogies and to find out more occasions for students for on job training. Fortunately that was the time when Prof. B.B. Pande joined Lucknow University as a Professor of Law and when I tried to implement Prof. Menon's approach in our university, Prof. Pande not only provided motivation but also guidance to see Law and Legal Process as a social institution and to understand how best Law may be used for the betterment and the development of the society. Of course, the interdisciplinary approach and clinical programmes were considered to be an essential part of the curriculum. After that, Lucknow University initiated several programmes successfully and I also got the share of my credit which was not mine because I was charged by a visionary like Prof. Menon and the real credit goes to him.

Prof. Menon has revolutionized the Indian Legal Education and he is a *karmayogi* in true sense. Now we have institutions of excellence in Indian Legal Education because of enduring partnership between the Humanities and Law initiated by Prof. Menon. It has been a stormy voyage but a very fruitful and rewarding one. Each time I have met Prof. Menon, it has broadened the vistas of mind in terms of acquiring new skills, learning the latest in not only the field of Law but specialization in Information Technology and other fast developing areas. His academic/ intellectual brilliance truly reflects his creativity in every institution which he has headed or in any activity which he has conducted and the effects of his words of wisdom on the legal fraternity. I am happy that I have worked with him in Ford Foundation project. It was really a learning experience when I prepared a report entitled "Criminal Justice System in Uttar Pradesh". I was benefited immensely during my stay at Bhopal in the neighbourhood of National Judicial Academy where he was the Director and he often advised me for bringing innovation in Legal Education. I know a lot of awards have been conferred on him but I think the persons who got the opportunity to be in his core association like Prof. Joga Rao, Prof. N.L. Mitra, Prof. Matthew, Prof. Ranvir Singh, Prof. K.D. Rao, Prof. Shri Krishna and many more who could transform and are now contributing towards law, legal education and the society. Prof. Menon has not only created institutions but also the human resource to manage those institutions.

I always feel secure and comfortable in his presence and I wish that he continues to shower his blessings on all of us. On completion of his 50 years of teaching, I salute him and wish that God may give him good health, strength and peace of mind so that he may continue to work for the Indian Legal Education.

PROF. BALRAJ CHAUHAN
Vice-Chancellor,
Dr. Ram Manohar Lohiya
National Law University,
Lucknow

MY IMPRESSIONS ABOUT DR. N.R. MADHAVA MENON

In 1988, when Dr. Madhava Menon established the National Law School of India University at Bangalore, I was fortunate to be one of the few to be associated with it. Dr. Menon had selected nine of us to be part of the law school at the initial stage. It was a Herculean task for Dr. Menon to build up the law school with meagre financial resources and practically nil infrastructure facilities, but he took it as a challenge with a determination to give a new thrust and direction to legal education in the country.

The school, when started, was located in the central college compound in Bangalore with three make-shift classrooms, one small auditorium-cum-seminar hall and a few cubicles for the director, faculty and staff. Infrastructure-wise, the facilities were far from satisfactory. But we had a dedicated and committed faculty and staff who worked hard under the strict guidance of a *"hard task master"*.

Dr. Menon's consistent enthusiasm and initiative was a source of inspiration and incentive for us, his team, to put-in maximum efforts to attain his vision to establish *a law school with a difference* – and not *yet another law school* as he always used to refer to it.

Dr. Menon has been a role model for all of us who worked with him as well as for those who knew him closely. His honesty and integrity, his punctuality, discipline and hard work were a guiding force which triggered our enthusiasm and initiative. His honesty and integrity was reflected even in the admission process which was done purely on merit and never did he succumb to any sort of pressure, political or otherwise. He wanted these attributes, the essential prerequisites for the legal profession, to be inculcated in the faculty and students. I still remember the statement he made in the first faculty meeting we had before the commencement of the classes for the first batch of students. *"All of you should go to the class as soon as the bell rings. If I find any class without a teacher, I will engage the class and then please don't feel embarrassed"*, he said. It worked. All of us were in our respective classes on the dot.

Dr. Menon has had a special technique to make us work. He would tell us what he expected from us, but would not compel us to do it. On the contrary, he would make us feel compelled to do it by himself demonstrating how to do it. For instance, after allocating the courses to be taught by each one of us, he asked me to prepare 50 topics (initially we had only 50 students in the first batch) under the Law of Torts and asked me to submit the same to him the next day. Since he had given me certain other assignments, I requested him to give me some more time. He just smiled and said, *"You try"*. Next day he came to my seat and asked me how much I could complete. I told him that I have prepared 20 topics. *"I have done it for you"*, he said and handed over the list of topics to me. I felt embarrassed, but it was a standing reminder for me to prioritize my assignments.

We started the law school with an initial intake of 50 students in the small campus with limited facilities. Within a span of three years, it has grown into a full fledged self-sufficient campus with well designed classrooms, state-of-the-art moot court hall, well equipped library & computer lab, hostel for boys and girls, facility for indoor and outdoor games, faculty quarters and a well furnished guest house for the visiting faculty. The growth has been instantaneous and enormous. The entire credit for this goes to Dr. Menon – his initiative, hard work and sincerity of purpose.

Working under Dr. Menon was a tremendous learning experience. From Nigeria, where I was picked-up by Dr. Menon, to Bangalore was a complete transformation from *leisure* to *hard work*. The students of the new law school were demanding and the teaching methods were innovative and interesting. The cooperative teaching method which Dr. Menon introduced in some courses, turned-out to be intellectually stimulating and extremely rewarding. After some initial reluctance, because of the fear of being exposed in the presence of our colleagues, we decided to try it on an experimental basis. Although it involved a lot of extra reading and pre-class discussions, in the process we learnt from each other as well as from the students' interactions and searching questions. The courses where we had adopted cooperative teaching as a method of teaching became very popular in due course.

My association with Dr. Madhava Menon was a turning point in my life. I am highly indebted to him for shaping my career as a law teacher. I owe him a lot for my present position as the Director of Amity Law School.

June 28, 2009.

PROF. M.K. BALACHANDRAN
Director, Amity Law School, Delhi

A TRUE 'KARMAYOGI'

It is with great pleasure and love I share my experience with Professor Madhava Menon, the Vice-Chancellor, NUJS, Kolkata. I am associated with Prof. Menon since 1988, from the days of making of NLSIU, Banglore. A very active, enthusiastic legal academic administrator he has been. I am intentionally using these words to describe him because he has been very dynamic, progressive and a hard task master. Compared to the age and time when he took over the charge at NUJS, Kolkata he completed his stint at NLSIU, Banglore and made his mark in the Nation by organising much needed changes in legal education. Study of law was almost a joke in the country everywhere, the metamorphosis designed by Menon & Co, gave legal education a new lease of life, a new zeal, and the much desired right direction and esteem.

Prof. Menon gave a clarion call to law students, law scholars and law teachers to join the mission for building new India with respect for law and it was the starting point for love for legal education, respect for legal studies and enthusiasm for legal research bloomed among the serious minded law scholars and educationists. A new morale started germinating among law teachers. He quickly facilitated and provided opportunity to many in the field to advance and sharpen their professional skills. Many young law teachers have undertaken their refresher course at NLSIU during 1989-90, 1990-91, 1991-92,1992-93 and reaped the benefit. And today most of the teachers exposed to NLSIU and Prof. Menon during the time are now in the helm of affairs in the country and also outside India. I fortunately belong to that group. Soon NLSIU apart from imparting standard legal education also integrated the law teachers of the country and a new brand of teachers took the task of disseminating the legal knowledge at their respective institutions irrespective of constraints and difficulties. The National Law School, Banglore has unfolded a new regime in legal education.

For Prof. Menon the work and compensation for the work at NUJS was backed up by a sense of fulfillment; he loved his work, he remained totally absorbed and lost in the affairs of the university, he never spent his time in any thing else. He used to come to office with the clock clicking 9.00 am along with a bottle of jira water and small tiffin box for lunch. He also used to bring a bunch of note sheets, books and assignments for colleagues. He used to have a full load of home work and never done anything without constructive application of mind. He is an excellent organizer; he never used to call us to his chamber, rather he visited our room with the assignments and tasks for us to perform and get back to him. He never minced his words about his expectations, he knew probably our potential and capacity accordingly he put us to maximum efficiency. Though he was satisfied with the team that he has picked up for making NUJS, he rarely expressed it and he has his own style of acknowledging his satisfaction. Being a strict disciplinarian and a great teacher, he himself is much disciplined. The chapters from his life and style provide volumes for a law teacher to learn, inculcate and reap success in life. He is a tireless person, he loved to take classes, he loved to be an active participant in seminars, he loved to write and generate legal research for future research. He had a great zeal in providing training to bureaucrats, judges, professionals and legislators with one secret goal of developing a honest, learned work culture and realize the dictates of our sacred constitution. He is a true 'karmayogi' in thoughts and deeds.

I had the opportunity to be a co-teacher with Prof. Menon in addressing classes with co-operative teaching method. I shared the very first class at NUJS with him and the class was packed with all students, teachers and some parents (of the students who missed the orientation programme) too. The class turned out to be one of the best lectures I have ever heard in my life. The trick of Prof. Menon was that it was not a class for the students but also the teachers to understand what is expected from them. I remember some of the parents of the students who were judges, eminent lawyers and administrative officers expressing their pleasure by reiterating that they should have joined as students again to learn lessons from Prof. Menon; such was the enchanting, mesmerizing impact on the audience. Prof. Menon's versatile style has been to convey message to different groups of listeners their lessons in one go. His classes provided learning opportunity not only for the students but also for the teachers. He always inspired all of us to be creative and original in our methods, skills and of course with an open mind to others.

He taught us to respect our adversaries more than our friends, for there is a great opportunity for learning. He taught us to be more democratic and accept the majority verdict with all humility. He never taught us by word but by his actions. One such instance is still fresh in memory. It was in the year 2001.

Professor Menon honestly believed that para-legal education course can provide great opportunities to those who desire to join as law clerks or corporate legal executives and for them undergoing full length professional course is unnecessary and counter-productive. Many corporate houses also had requested him to provide such human resource for their organization. Enthused by such belief and assurance from business houses, Menon had undertaken a very monotonous project of designing the course, syllabus, regulations, and build up necessary supporting documents to get a positive nod from the General Council, NUJS. Prof. Menon prepared for the final presentation with all minor and technical things taken care of and he presented the theme before the Lord Chancellor, Mr. Justice A.S. Anand, the then Chief Justice of India. The matter was listened and without any debate the ruling came 'the project has to wait for some time as the University is loaded with its basic commitments to pursue'. The matter rested there to our great surprise. For us it was Prof. Menon's much loved project versus the Chancellor's negation; we could not accept the decision, but the Vice-Chancellor Prof. Menon whispered to us 'let us honour the authority and accept the ruling with all humility'. Alas! The project almost died, and it is not going to happen in near future, probably, the project was much ahead of its time or India missed one good opportunity. To conceive a project is one thing while executing the project is another task in Indian conditions—Menon could have provided another great vista to legal knowledge, legal education and legal scholarship.

The awards and rewards whatever the nation gave him are minuscule; he has the vision and capacity to look to the nation and mankind in wholesomeness and can contribute very meaningfully. Prof. Menon is a tough task master. He has the art of getting the best in every teacher, staff and students; he has the skill in developing the personality of a staff to one's completeness. Most of the time for this reason, he is misunderstood and some colleagues felt difficult to work with him; and some of the acquaintances felt they need to get relieved of him, but on later analysis most realized they missed a great and good opportunity. I feel most of the critics of Prof. Menon either did not understand him or his work style where he has always been a giver rather than taker. He upgraded many precious legal human resource of the country. He created many good judges, lawyers, academicians, corporate lawyers, law clerks and I had the opportunity of meeting quite few of them and all have praises for the learning they had from him.

As a teacher, I have learnt many a lesson from Prof.Menon, and I always consider there is still lot to learn from him; his commitment, his involvement, his sacrifices, his urge to always give something, his happiness in reading, learning and disseminating knowledge, his scholarship, his method of presenting, and his contentment with whatever he has done.

He always used to say that for all the hard work that one does as a teacher no amount of money can compensate, but the compensation if at all, it is sense of fulfillment at the end of the day. Professor Menon to his credit has many accomplished works and he is very content person. Yet there is zeal and hunger in him that he can still serve the Nation and mankind. Prof. Menon rendered his service as Vice-Chancellor of NUJS without taking any salary or allowances from the University – a great service indeed. I feel very happy and enchanting to be associated with such versatile personality.

Kolkata
June 15, 2009.

PROF. (DR.) BHAVANI PRASAD PANDA
WB National University of
Juridical Sciences (NUJS), Kolkata

SAGA OF A SAGE

It is love for him and of him that mutually construct admiration for Professor N R Madhava Menon. For many, of whom yours truly is one, he is a person to be respected, obeyed, and admired – all from a distance. Yet, his presence in their lives is amazingly intimate, soothing, comforting and total; like a huge tree overhead.

The life-time achievements of Prof. Menon are only partial reflection of his unbounded energy. Sheer quantity of his intellectual output and continuity of their flow are awesome. And if the wideness of acceptance of his voluminous work across the intellectual fraternity is any indication, Prof Menon has his place on firm footing among greatest educators of our time. Yet, he is more magnanimous than the monuments of his achievement, from which he draws off again and again in saintly detachment to move forward in life and action.

My association with him was relatively recent, in comparison to his innumerable students and older colleagues from early sixties. It was only in November 2000 that I had come to his direct contact, through my job of a finance and accounts personnel in the National University of Juridical Sciences, and continued till September 2003, when he left NUJS to join the NJA. Hardly did I then realize that his affection, care and concern (permit me to call it love) will be so pervasive; encompassing lives of each member of my family.

I am not his student nor can I claim to be his colleague in any academic sense. Yet, he is my true teacher-philosopher who baptized me into the process of unlearning what was not contextually relevant to my profession and taught some of the basic traits that add value to life. He once told me that in an educational institution, the first stake-holder of it is its students and any measure of financial propriety should begin and end with identifying what is beneficial to them. That learning process is still on.

I distinguish myself among his admirers in two ways. One, my interactions with him rounded essentially on administrative matters, which was far more restricted and formal as compared to the width and intensity normally commanded by teacher-student and fellow academic relationships. In spite of that, I find myself blessed with his affection in no lesser measure. In fact, it goes much beyond what I deserve. The other is that I had the unique privilege of living for a considerable length of time in the same apartment house of Banashree Abasan, Salt Lake, Kolkata; his flat being on the floor just above mine (My wife used to describe the Menons as the God and the Goddess overhead.) Self composed and private as the Menons are, this neighbourhood proximity provided glimpses of their disciplined personal habits. I have come to believe that the real Prof Menon is more identifiable in his spirituality and naturally composed personality than in the volumes of his scholastics and research.

Dear readers and fellow admirers, kindly permit me to recount two incidents involving Prof. Menon that underline his quality as a human being.

On 26th of January, 2003, the day the conferment of Padmashree on him was announced; Prof. and Mrs. Menon were at Deoghar, in Jharkhand, on a private visit. They were expected to return by the same evening, but could reach home after midnight, amidst unseasonal rain and biting cold. When I met him on the stairway, he told that the car they were traveling broke down on the way in an uninhabited place and it had been hours before any help could reach. Sensing that he was still unaware of the award, I congratulated him on the conferment. For a moment, he seemed instantly surprised at the unexpected announcement, only to regain his usual composure and took it on a light vein. He asked, "Whom do I thank? The God or the President?" I gathered enough courage to reply that the first take of it should go to me, for I was awake till that unholy hour to congratulate him. His next question, also on the same lighter vein, was, "What do they do with the Padmashrees? Is there any tax relief or something of the sort?" This is Prof. Menon, the humble person unmoved by worldly recognition and glory.

I saw the same Prof. Menon visibly upset when he came to know that a casual worker of M/S Bridge and Roof, the construction firm then building the NUJS Campus, fell from a considerable height at the site of work and sustained severe head injury. He called up everyone including ministers and secretaries of the Government, besides pressing the entire administration of NUJS, in securing all possible medical aid.

Despite his efforts, the life of the person could not be saved. I will never forget the face of Prof. Menon, all in pains, when the news was broken to him. It was compassion at its divine best.

My recollection will remain incomplete without a mention of Mrs. Rema Menon, who is his perfect consort in the imperfect world he lives. In many ways they make a strange couple. Mrs. Menon is deeply religious, seclusive, homely and soft, the attributes Prof. Menon is not exactly known for. A poet at heart, she likes to see the world in her own way and prefers a quiet life for themselves in Kerala. Prof. Menon is constantly dragged out to live in places she does not enjoy; be it Kolkata, Bhopal or Delhi. Yet she braves out the pain of her arthritis to shift over time and again to places with unkind weather conditions that aggravate her ailment. Yet they are very close, sharing together every single moment of their life. A self-made and complete person as the Professor is known in the outside world, his lady has lasting contribution and silent sacrifice over the past five decades and more to this making.

For the last so many years, the couple has been dreaming to retire permanently to the place of Guruvayur, their very own temple town in Kerala. It has not materialized the way they earnestly longed for. May God grant them that and long life of peace and health.

June 10, 2009.

D. KANUNJNA
Former Finance Officer
NUJS, Kolkata

MY BEST TEACHER[1]

I joined the Faculty of Law as a lecturer in 1985 when I first met Professor N.R. Madhava Menon, who was faculty-in-charge at that time. I had the opportunity to work closely with him and learn how to blend administrative work and academic activities. He was focused on promoting and introducing innovations in legal education. But he never spoke in a vacuum and substantiated any thought by doing sufficient home work on it. He didn't believe in merely passing on the orders to others but took the initiative of doing things himself.

Time management and maintaining a diary of daily work are two among the many things that I have learnt from him. I find it highly beneficial now, when I have to juggle between administrative and academic work, writing papers, interacting with students and attending conferences across the globe.

For him, the welfare of students was of paramount importance. He used to say, 'If we have opted for teaching after leaving our practice, where one could have earned much more, then we should be passionate about imparting education.'

He has been a constant support to me over the years and has been continuously encouraging me to undertake different responsibilities. Even today, I rely on him and seek his advice wherever I want to initiate something new. When I had prepared the law curriculum for Guru Gobind Singh Indraprastha University (GGSIPU), I had a discussion with him and had incorporated many new things on his suggestion.

I am highly inspired by his energy. He is in his '70s now and still works so much. He has made me realize that all of us have inner energy, we just need to channelise it in the right direction.

DR. NOMITA AGGARWAL
Dean and HoD, Faculty of Law
Delhi University

1. Courtesy: The Times of India, Delhi.

Prof. Menon and Mrs. Rema Menon on the occasion of 44th marriage anniversary on 8th July 2009

The Menon Family: Mrs. Rema Menon, Son R.K Menon, Daughter-in-law Mrs. Anuradha Menon, Grandsons Ajay and Vijay

The Menon family in 1984, son Ramesh and daughter Devi

H.E. Dr. A.P.J. Abdul Kalam conferring The National Honour Padma Shree on Prof. Menon in April 2009

Outside Rashtrapati Bhawan after receiving Padma Shree
with Mrs. Menon and elder sister Dr. Sarojini Amma

नीलकण्ट रामकृष्ण माधव मेनोन्

मैं, भारत का राष्ट्रपति, आ.प.जै. अब्दुल कलाम, व्यक्तिगत गुणों के लिए आपके सम्मानार्थ, पद्म श्री प्रदान करता हूँ।

कलाम
राष्ट्रपति

नई दिल्ली
दिनांक 13 चैत्र, 1925
3 अप्रैल, 2003

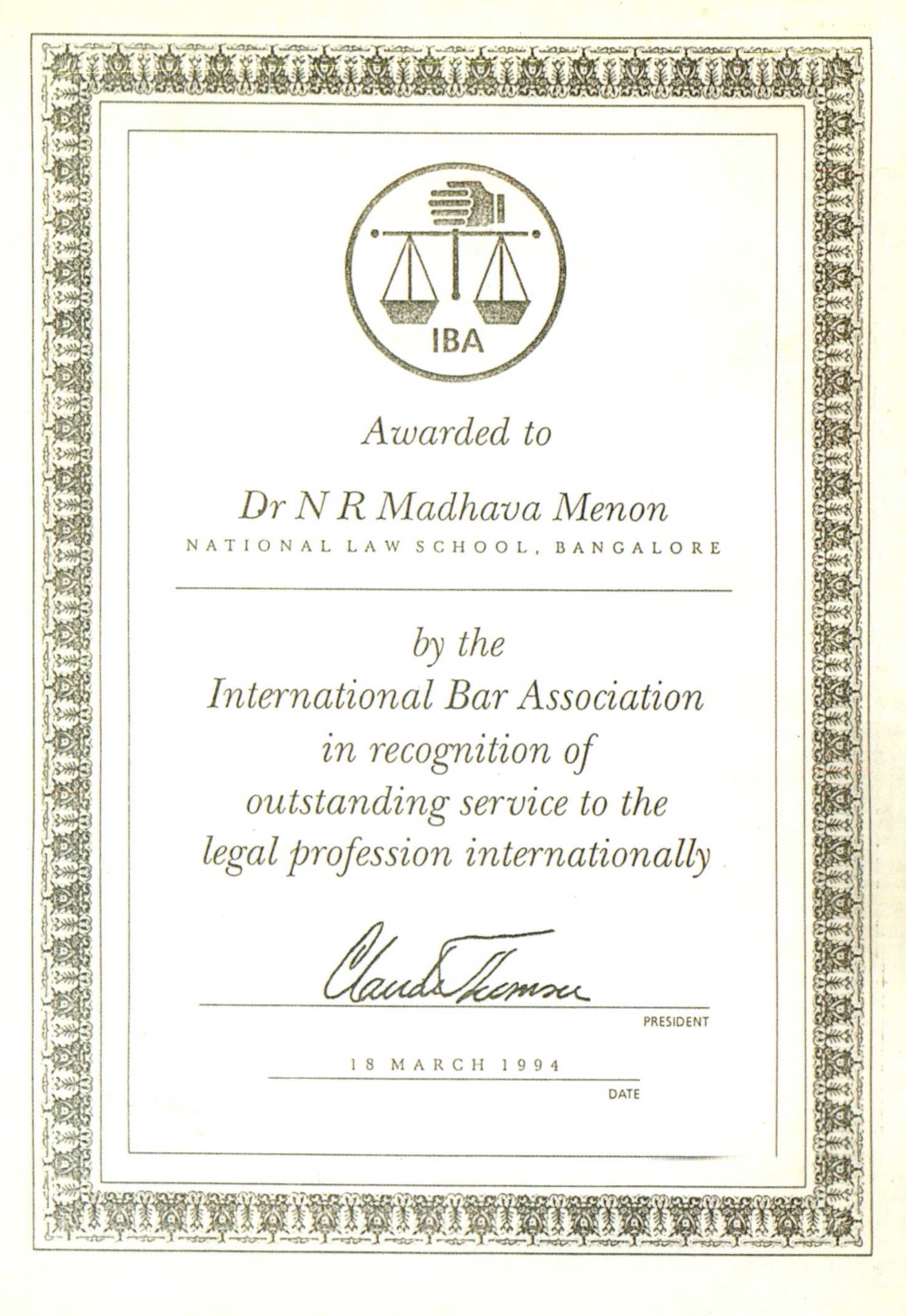

International Bar Association recognizes
Dr. Menon's Outstanding service to Legal profession
internationally by an award in 1994

CJEI Commonwealth Judicial Education Institute

Commonwealth Judicial Education Institute

In the cherished memory and grateful remembrance of

The Right Honourable Telford Georges O.C.C.

for his landmark lifetime contribution to Judicial Administration and Judicial Education throughout the Commonwealth.

This award is bestowed on

Dr. N. R. Madhava Menon,

Director of the National Judicial Academy of India

Given under our hands and seal

This 14th day of March A.D., 2005

The Rt. Honourable
Chief Justice Sir Dennis Byron
President

Sandra E. Oxner, O.C.
Chairperson

Dr. L.M. Singhvi
Patron

Commonwealth Judicial Education Institute, Halifax, Canada recognises Dr. Menon's land mark contribution to Judicial Education throughout the Commonwealth in March 2005

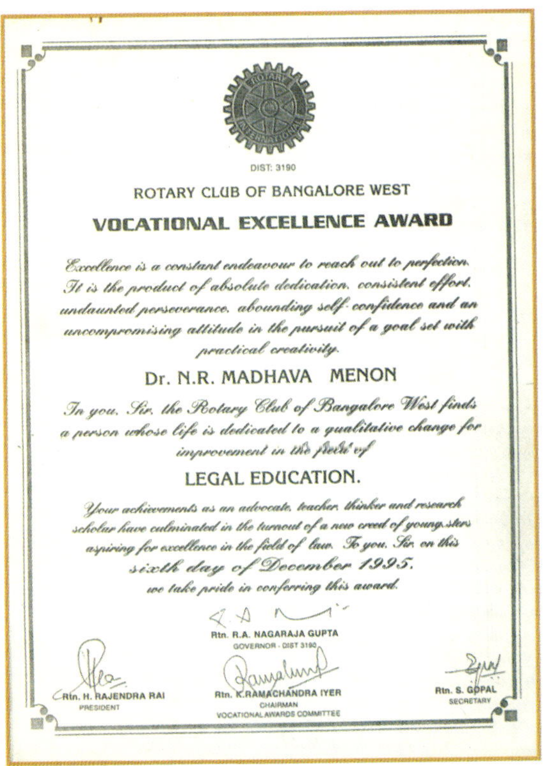

ROTARY INTERNATIONAL

DIST: 3190

ROTARY CLUB OF BANGALORE WEST

VOCATIONAL EXCELLENCE AWARD

Excellence is a constant endeavour to reach out to perfection. It is the product of absolute dedication, consistent effort, undaunted perseverance, abounding self-confidence and an uncompromising attitude in the pursuit of a goal set with practical creativity.

DR. N.R. MADHAVA MENON

To you, Sir, the Rotary Club of Bangalore West finds a person whose life is dedicated to a qualitative change for improvement in the field of

LEGAL EDUCATION.

Your achievements as an advocate, teacher, thinker and research scholar have culminated in the turnout of a new creed of youngsters aspiring for excellence in the field of law. To you, Sir, on this sixth day of December 1995, we take pride in conferring this award.

Rtn. R.A. NAGARAJA GUPTA
GOVERNOR - DIST 3190

Rtn. H. RAJENDRA RAI
PRESIDENT

Rtn. K. RAMACHANDRA IYER
CHAIRMAN
VOCATIONAL AWARDS COMMITTEE

Rtn. S. GOPAL
SECRETARY

Rotary Club, Bangalore honours Dr. Menon with Vocational Excellence Award, 1995 for turning legal education on the path of excellence

Receiving the Living Legend of Law Award from the President of International Bar Association

With Justice A.S. Anand, Justice M.N. Venkatachaliah former Chief Justice of India at the 9th Convocation of NLSIU, Bangalore

With Justice Michael Kirby, High Court of Australia, Justice Mehmud, Chief Justice of South Africa, Chief Justices of India Justice J.S. Verma and E.S. Venkatramiah at the 5th Convocation of NLSIU, Bangalore

At the Workshop on Constitutional Litigation with Mr. Justice Jeevan Reddy, Mr. Soli J. Sorabjee, Mr. Justice V.R. Krishna Iyer and Mr. Ram Jethmalani

With former President of India Dr. A.P.J. Abdul Kalam
at the National Law School Convocation

At Farewell Function for Mrs. and Mr. Menon on relinquishing office as Director, NLSIU in 1997 with Director N.L. Mitra, Mrs. Mitra and Chief Justice J.S. Verma

Menon as Captain of the Horse Riding Club of Aligarh Muslim University in 1962

As student at Law College, Trivandrum

The Horse Riding Team with
Prime Minister Sri Jawaharlal Nehru in 1962

With the President of India Dr. Zakir Hussain

When Aligarh University Law Students met Prime Minister Mrs. Indira Gandhi

At the time of wedding in 1965

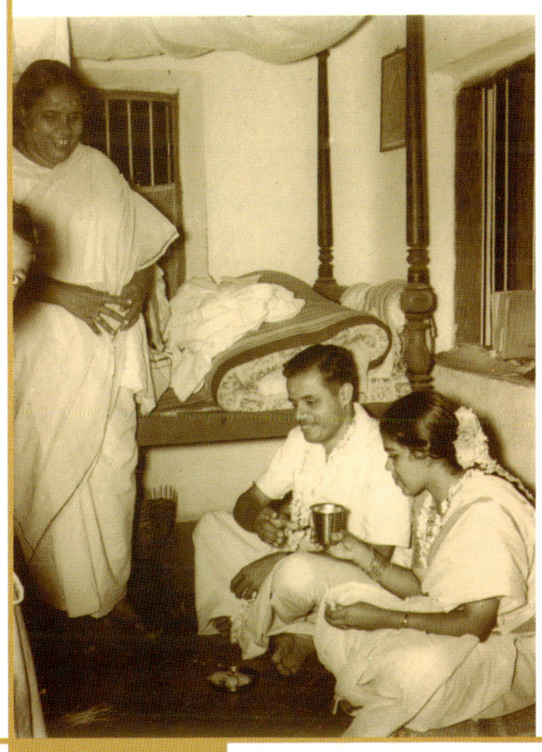

Exchange of milk ceremony on entering home after marriage while Dr. Menon's mother, T.G. Bhawani Amma looks on

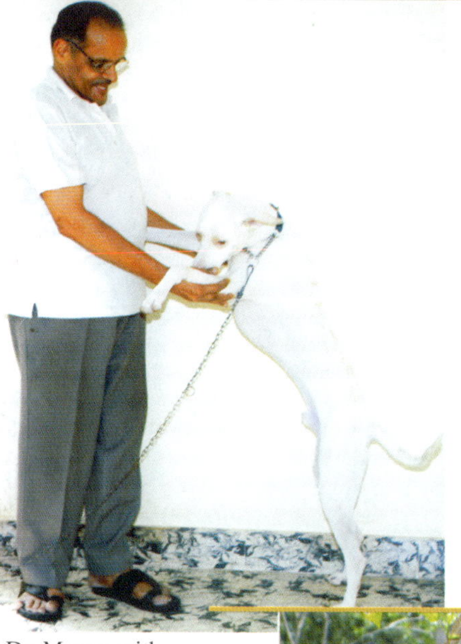

Dr. Menon with
his pet Raja

Dr. Menon with his pet dog Daniel at his home in Trivandrum

Dr. Menon at South African Zoo